OUR STORY

A Memoir of Love and Life in China

Rao Pingru

Translated from the Chinese by Nicky Harman

SQUARE PEG

10 9 8 7 6 5 4 3 2 1

Square Peg, an imprint of Vintage,
20 Vauxhall Bridge Road,
London SW1V 2SA

Square Peg is part of the Penguin Random House group of companies
whose addresses can be found at global.penguinrandomhouse.com

 Penguin
Random House
UK

Published in the UK by Square Peg in 2018
First published in China as *Pingru meitang: Wo lia de gushi* by
Guangxi Normal University Press, Guilin in 2013

penguin.co.uk/vintage

A CIP catalogue record for this book is available from the British Library

ISBN 9781910931752

Cover design by Janet Hanson
Book design by Maggie Hinders

This book has been selected to receive financial assistance from English
PEN's "PEN Translates!" programme, supported by Arts Council England.
English PEN exists to promote literature and our understanding of it, to
uphold writers' freedoms around the world, to campaign against the
persecution and imprisonment of writers for stating their views, and to
promote the friendly co-operation of writers and the free exchange of
ideas. www.englishpen.org

Printed and Bound by Toppan Leefung Printing Ltd

Penguin Random House is committed to a sustainable future for our
business, our readers and our planet. This book is made from Forest
Stewardship Council® certified paper.

Every word I have written is true

Every story is true

All these pictures of the past

Came from my head

CONTENTS

OUR STORY

Those moments could have become treasured memories,
but regrettably we were each
happily absorbed in our own young lives in those days.

1
Our Childhood Years

PINGRU

My first clear memories are of the ceremony that marked the formal start of my schooling. I was eight years old.

First, the right day had to be chosen. When it arrived, I was woken by a servant at about three o'clock in the morning. I washed and dressed, and went to the main hall of our house, where everything was prepared: my father, mother, and the gentleman who was to initiate me into the mysteries of education were standing by the tablet that honored Confucius. In the stillness of the night, the candlelight lent an air of great solemnity to the occasion, and I felt a thrill of excitement. But what really made me happy were the Four Treasures of Study, the brand-new brush, ink, paper, and inkstone laid out on the writing desk. The gentleman in question was my "Uncle Huang," and we were related by marriage: his eldest daughter was married to my big brother. His full name was Huang Xiaopu and he was at that time chief judge at the Hunan Province Supreme Court. His calligraphy was beautiful. He grasped my hand and together we traced the first lesson: lines of characters dedicated to the greatest educator of all, Confucius. He gripped my hand painfully hard, but I did not dare make a sound.

It was the custom for the very first characters written during this ceremony to be put away carefully by one's mother. Afterward, we went to the sitting room, where an array of drinks and food were laid out down one side of the room. The steam which rose from the dishes of hot food seemed especially designed to dispel the seriousness of the moment. After our meal, my big brother took me to school. As we walked through the silent streets, the first light of dawn was visible in the sky. It was bitingly cold.

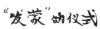

The initiation ceremony

The sign on the table reads: "Confucius, our most revered teacher."

描红时之情景

Tracing the characters

"描红纸"的式样

The characters that I had to trace

大哥带我去上小学

My big brother took me to school.

Father's bowl   Mother's bowl

After I began school, I was required to fill my parents' bowls with rice at every meal.
Two lessons taught to me by my parents that I never forgot were, one, to respect and value any
paper with writing on it, and, two, to respect and value the food we ate. Every scrap of food
had to be eaten, and on no account should even a grain of rice be dropped on the floor.
"Never forget the effort that's gone into producing every grain of rice, and every thread of silk," I was told.

That was our first year in Nanchang city. My father was a lawyer and we lived in a house by Chenjia Bridge. It was not a good location, but there were complicated reasons why we were there: my father's younger sister had married a man from a wealthy family. But unbeknownst to her family, the man to whom she had been given in marriage was in poor health, and, scarcely a year later, she was widowed and mother to a baby daughter, my cousin. For this reason, my father was determined to take good care of his younger sister. One evening when my cousin was five, on the anniversary of her father's death, her nanny, a fearsome old woman, took the little girl to the ceremonies that were being carried out to placate his spirit.

妈妈教我怎样洗脸：
「耳朵背、后颈窝」

我大概左10岁

左右开始学习
自己洗脸。我顾
名思义，把脸洗好
放下毛巾就想走，
妈妈不允许，要我
把日耳朵背、后颈
窝这两个部位洗
干净、才能走。
她边教我拧干毛
巾的手法：男子应遮
右手左上，左手在下；女子则
反之。顺时钟方向。如果男子甫女
子的手法，别人要
笑你的。

女式

男式

OPPOSITE

I have forgotten most of the things my mother said to me. But one dictum still rings in my ears: "Wash behind your ears, and the nape of your neck."

Mother taught me that washing my face also meant washing behind the ears, and the back of the neck.

I was about ten when I first began to wash my face for myself. I took it to mean just my face, so I washed it, put down the washcloth, and was ready to go. But Mother would not allow that: "Wash behind your ears, and the nape of your neck," she commanded. And only when those two places were clean would she let me leave.

Then she taught me how to wring out the washcloth: for a boy, it was right hand on top, left hand below, and wring clockwise (bottom right). For a girl, it was the opposite (bottom left). If you were a boy and did it the girl's way, everyone laughed at you.

Chenjia Bridge in the 1930s

午餐桌上的大家庭

The family at dinner

Clockwise from bottom, center: Mother, Pingru, Father, Father's cousin, Big Brother, Niece, Second Nephew, Big Brother's wife, Eldest Nephew, Grandmother, Second (elder) Sister, Third (younger) Brother

母亲在晚饭后给我和弟弟讲故事

After dinner, my mother would tell stories to me and my younger brother.

"Go on! Go and see! Your daddy's come!" The old woman screamed at my cousin and pushed her forward. My cousin was so traumatized by this experience that she lost her wits. Although she did marry and have children, she was never happy.

My aunt had a relative who was investing in various ventures, and she borrowed 8,000 yuan to put in and became his partner. I do not know whether the ventures really lost money, but I do know that she was unable to pay the loan back. Then she mortgaged the house at Chenjia Bridge but was still unable to manage and asked my father to rent it from her. And that was why we spent eight years there.

After dinner every day, Third Brother and I (the two youngest children in the fam-

芦衣顺母

In threadbare clothes, he obeyed his stepmother.

ily) would go to my mother's bed, where she told us stories. They were mostly traditional tales about morality: about Min Ziqian,[1] who was obedient to his stepmother even though she treated him badly, and about Six-Feet Alley, the story of how a wise minister resolved a boundary dispute in Imperial China.[2] I still remember the emotion on her face as she got to the bit where Min Ziqian begs his father not to repudiate his cruel stepmother:

"If Mother stays at home, only I have to endure the cold. But if you divorce Mother, all three of us children will suffer the cold."

And her laughter as she explained the last two lines of "Six-Feet Alley."

上世纪40年代故乡南城的街景

A street scene in my family's hometown, Nancheng county, in the 1940s. From left to right, the shop signs read: "Meiliuli Rice Noodles," "Yi Shun Shen Pharmacy," "Dachang Fabrics," "Rice."

Our family was originally from Nancheng county, Fuzhou district, Jiangxi province. Nancheng dates back to ancient times, to the days when Liu Bang ruled as the first Han dynasty emperor, and Nancheng belonged to Yuzhang district.

The Xu River flowed north through old Nancheng; the town walls were built on the west bank of the river, and there were gates to the north, south, east, and west. Within the town, there was North Street, South Street, East Street, and West Street. The last was the longest. Our home was on North Street. The east bank was the outskirts of

Map showing Nancheng county

Clockwise, from top right: Anhui province (yellow), Fujian province (gray), Guangdong province (purple), Hunan province (green), Hubei province (blue), Jiangxi province (orange, in center). The city marked by a double circle is Nanchang, the provincial capital. The town marked by a red dot is Nancheng, Pingru's birthplace.

the town, so once you crossed Peace Bridge, there was less to see and fewer people around. The town and surrounding countryside were crisscrossed with waterways, like the veins of a leaf, and encircled by serried ranks of beautiful jade-green peaks. Among the most famous were Magu Mountain and Conggu Mountain. There is a Song dynasty poem which goes

Flourishing fields of wheat and green, green mountains, a winding road.
The land of the South, stretching a thousand li, brings tears to the eyes in spring.
Mother Xu stands at the river crossing, calls to the ferryman, points far off to the
    third valley, Mayuan.

Seen through a poet's eyes, the charm of my hometown had not changed much since the days of the Song dynasty: cocks crowed and dogs barked, the boatmen sang as they plied their oars, and the landscape of waterways and mountains had remained the same for generation after generation.

The "Mayuan" of the poem is the largest of the valleys of Magu Mountain, and legend has it that this is where Magu, the Hemp Goddess, practiced Daoism. Magu was a legendary Daoist immortal, apparently just a girl of eighteen or nineteen when she saw with her own eyes the bed of the East Sea rise up and turn into dry land and mulberry fields three times. No doubt I was influenced by the legend, because to my mind there was a cosmic feel about the Mayuan valley.

There was another reason why Mayuan was special to me: the land was very fertile— it was where the so-called silver pearl or cold water white rice was cultivated—and my mother bought a piece of land there and put the title deed in my name. I never saw it firsthand but my father told me it was about twenty mu (three acres). Mayuan valley was also where my father's father was buried. After my mother died, she was buried beside my grandfather, to his left, in a slightly smaller grave. In 1958, the local government built a reservoir in the valley; the mulberry fields really did become an azure sea, and the two graves vanished beneath its waters.

OPPOSITE

Nancheng delicacies in the 1930s and 1940s
Lye zongzi dumplings

TOP For the zongzi, lye was added to the best-quality glutinous rice (the lye was apparently made by burning rice straw to ash, but I do not know for certain). The glutinous rice mixture, which was quite bulky, was tightly wrapped in leaves and steamed until soft and pale yellow. We ate these fragrant dumplings dipped in brown sugar, and they were quite delicious.

Soup vermicelli

BOTTOM Good-quality japonica rice was used to make tender vermicelli, which was served in a tasty soup with meat and vegetables. The traditional way of serving the vermicelli: each person had a shallow soup bowl, with about one ounce of boiled rice noodles, the same quantity of soup was added, and scallion tips were sprinkled on top. When you finished that, you could go back for another helping. A healthy young person often had five or six servings. The waiters added up the bill by counting the bowls. It tasted different from vermicelli soup served from one large bowl. Sadly, the old way of serving the vermicelli in individual bowls has now vanished, as I discovered on my 2010 trip back to Nancheng.

故乡南城的"美食"

上世纪三四十年代

石碱 粽子

用精选之糯米加
"碱水"(据说以稻
草灰为原料,未知
其详)制作。体验
稍大,扎得紧,煮得
烂,呈金黄色,食
时清香扑鼻,佐
以红糖,口感极
佳。

此种吃法与大碗汤粉
现在已经消失,二〇一〇年曾去南
城,此法失传矣,可惜。

汤粉

用上等粳米制成粉条,
极细嫩,汤有荤(精肉)
素(豆豉)之分,均极鲜美。
传统食法,用普通扁平菜
碗,内盛滚热之米粉一两左右,
加入相当比例的汤,再加葱姜
末,吃毕再来一碗。青壮年一
顿吃五六碗乃是常事。堂倌(服
务员也)只数碗便可算出费用。

For ordinary people in Nancheng, life was as lively as it always had been in such fertile regions. My grandfather wrote a poem about it:

> The husband has gone to Ningzhou to buy green tea, the wife plants new squash
>   behind the ferry landing.
> The boy, with no work to do, rows to a mossy bank by night, lights pine resin,
>   plays at will-o'-the-wisp.

There were four distinct seasons in Nancheng. In the words of the Song dynasty monk-poet Hui Kai: "White flowers in spring, the moon in autumn, cool breezes in summer, snow in winter. If you have no cares, then all the seasons are good." A child has no cares, and, during holidays, times really were good. Whether it was the Grave-Sweeping Festival, the Start of Summer, the Dragon Boat Festival, the Double Seventh, the Midautumn Festival, or the Double Ninth, there would be much more food and drink than normal. And this was probably the chief reason why we children loved festivals.

In Nancheng county, there was a traditional way of celebrating the Start of Summer Festival, called "Push into Summer." As the rhyme went: "Push hard into summer, push hard into summer, raise your energy." The character 撑, cheng, which Nancheng folk pronounced with the fourth tone, meant "push in hard." The grown-ups would tell us, laughing: "You kids can eat as much as you like today, it's Push into Summer day. But after today, no more stuffing your faces!" After the Start of Summer Festival, the weather got a lot hotter and we ate less, and had lighter meals. The festival was marked by another folk custom too. In my family, it was called "the weigh-in": the cook and the driver brought out an enormous balance scales, and we boys, Third Brother and I, and Qingzeng and Shaozeng (my older brother's sons), were all put on it to be weighed. When summer was over, we were weighed again, we never knew quite why. I imagine that since we ate less in summer, we lost weight and were at risk of falling ill, and this was a way of confirming that we were in good health.

Girls did not need to be weighed, so my niece Yunqin was able to avoid the weigh-in.

At the Dragon Boat Festival, according to the county annals, there used to be dragon boat races held along the river by the Peace Bridge. They must have been lively affairs, but sadly I never saw them myself. The Dragon Boat Festival lye zongzi dumplings, however, left a big impression on me. In my family, we used to have something else for breakfast, and then eat our zongzi and hard-boiled eggs and garlic tops at noon. Lye water, made by filtering water through rice straw ash, was added to the glutinous rice grains. The dumplings were made by wrapping the rice in leaves and tying them tightly with string. These were then put in to cook. When they were soft, the dumplings were thick and solid, pale yellow in color. We ate them dipped in brown sugar, and they were indescribably delicious. Meitang and I both used to eat these when we were little, but for decades after we came to Shanghai, we never tasted them. Then in 2003, quite by chance, I saw them on sale in the Fuhua Lou store near our home and quickly bought some to share with Meitang. At that time, we felt that there was not enough lye in them, and they were not as tasty and sticky as they had been back home.

The evening of the Midautumn Festival, our family put a square table in the courtyard, covered by a crimson tablecloth on which were laid incense sticks, candles, and fruit. The centerpiece of course was the mooncakes. Nancheng mooncakes were thin and slightly flattened, about the diameter of a rice bowl, although there were bigger ones too. They were filled with rock candy, red and green candied fruit strips, walnuts, and ground-up melon seeds. White sesame seeds were scattered on top, and the character for month, 月, was written in black sesame seeds. If the mooncakes were a larger size, then the four characters for "Midautumn Mooncake," 中秋月饼, were written on them. They were hard and sweet, and had their own special flavor.

The festival that we children most enjoyed was Chinese New Year. For a whole month beforehand, the family was busy making preparations. First, we bought fish and meat for salting and curing. The food was prepared, and the house swept and cleaned, and every member of the family got new clothes. My little brother and I had long silk gowns made for us, generally in plain dark blue or green.

The evening of the twenty-third day of the twelfth lunar month, incense and candles were lit and my father would lead my brothers and me to the kitchen to pay our respects to the kitchen god. We set off firecrackers and scattered short lengths of rice straw mixed with millet. The belief was that the kitchen god worked there all through the year, keeping a close eye on what we did and how we behaved, until on this evening he got on his horse and rode up into the sky to deliver his report to the Jade Emperor. These broken bits of rice straw and millet were meant to feed his horse on its journey.

勧时在江西所吃的月饼

The mooncakes I ate as a child in Jiangxi

The largest cake is inscribed with the character for "moon," the four smaller cakes are each inscribed with one of the characters for "Midautumn Mooncakes."

This was a solemn ceremony, with the adults of the family calling out, "Ah . . . lu-lu-lu . . ." as they flung the straw into the air to encourage the horse to eat its fill and get the journey off to a good start.

We also made offerings to the kitchen god, including some of the local malt sugar. Malt sugar, made from rice, and sticky and sweet, was designed to sweeten his words in his report about us, so it was essential. All the same, to make quite sure he did not forget, we pasted reminders to the left and right of his effigy. The couplets read:

When you go to heaven, talk of our good deeds;
When you return to earth, bring us peace.

On the twenty-fourth of the twelfth lunar month, called the "little year," we ate vegetarian dishes and made offerings to the ancestors. By this time, we had been busy making preparations for two weeks or more, and everything was largely ready, so we could begin to enjoy the New Year celebrations.

For us children, this was the most enjoyable time of all—there was the delicious anticipation of a holiday that was imminent but had not yet arrived.

At the "little year," we were always given a bowl of "scalded meat and thread noodles" to eat. Thread noodles, a kind of vermicelli, and the meat, in the form of small meatballs, were placed in boiling water, then taken off the flame and served the instant they were cooked. Simple but good. These noodles are what I remember best of the "little year."

Later, when we were in Nanchang city, the best thing for us children was that we got to celebrate the New Year twice. Most people had their New Year's Eve dinner on the night of the thirtieth day of the lunar month, but my maternal grandmother's family had theirs on the twenty-seventh. My maternal grandfather, Yang Yichen, had immigrated to Nanchang from Guangxi, and that was why there was no clan memorial hall in Nanchang. I imagine that the reason their family celebrated New Year's Eve on the twenty-seventh was that they had brought the habit with them from somewhere in Guangxi.

On the morning of the twenty-seventh, my mother, my little brother, and I put on our new clothes and called two rickshaws—one of the pullers was always Old Yu and the other, one of his friends.[3] My maternal grandmother lived at Number 8, Xi Shu Yuan Street, once the mansion of a high government minister. Her husband and his three brothers had bought only one-third of it, but it was substantial. There were separate quarters for the four families, housing nearly a hundred people including the servants. My grandmother occupied the large room on the east side of the main hall. We wished her a happy New Year and received our gift money. This we handed over to our mother for safekeeping, perfectly happy with the two or three silver dollars we were allowed to keep in our pockets. Then Third Brother and I ran off to amuse ourselves, either reading my older cousin's *Little Friend* magazines or playing games in the small garden on the east side of my grandmother's room. For instance, we would break off dried sticks, build a house, and use it as a stable for a Tang pottery horse. Sometimes my mother would call us in to eat something, and then we'd go out again to play.

In the evening, we had our New Year's meal. Our grandmother did not join us; she ate separately in her own quarters. We gathered around a large round table in a room behind the main hall, with my uncles and aunts and their families. Tenth Uncle enjoyed literary jokes. Once, he placed a large morsel of red-cooked pork in my bowl and declaimed some lines from a Li Bai poem: "A great piece provides inspiration for one's writing!" "A great piece" originally referred to a large piece of land, but here he meant the pork. Once I had eaten that, my aunt, who was sitting opposite me, picked up long strands of bean vermicelli and put them in my bowl too: "Pingru! Long strands, long visits!"

Once we had finished our meal, we went in family groups to pay our respects to the ancestors in the great hall at the rear of the complex. Palace lanterns hung in every room of the house, and the great hall was the most brilliantly illuminated of all. Incense smoke curled into the air, and huge red candles were placed before niches that held the ancestral tablets and portraits hand-embroidered on silk. The hall was crowded with uncles and aunts and cousins, young and old, all dressed in their finest clothes. In addition to the three sacrifices on the offerings table, there was a large rice pot, its round shape symbolizing family unity. The steaming rice was colored a lucky red, a miniature balance scales for weighing gold was inserted into it in its wooden case, and other auspicious snacks, such as peanuts, jujubes, and longans, were scattered on top. When the ceremony began, gongs were struck and firecrackers set off, and the rafters rang with the noise. And with these splendid festivities, the curtain came down on the old year in my maternal grandmother's family.

The thirtieth day of the lunar year finally arrived. It was my father's job to write the New Year couplets. He penned them on the last day of the old year and pasted them up on the morning of the first day of the new year. On the main gate, they read:

Shen Tu
Fu Lei

These were the formal names of the door gods. Any malign spirits or demons had only to read these august names and they would immediately take fright and disappear. The couplets had a most calming effect on the home. Then on the middle door, as one entered, there was another couplet:

Zhuge was careful and cautious his entire life.
Lü Duan addressed great matters with a clear mind.

Finally, as one went through the door into the house, there were my father's favorites:

Heaven causes time to pass, people increase in years.
As spring arrives, heaven and earth heap blessings on the family.

Thus, the couplets proceeded from heavenly personages to historic personages, and finally concerned the happiness of the family, so that the farther one advanced into the house, the more affectionate their tone became.

It was time to eat our New Year's meal. The whole family gathered around a large table. At the head of the table sat my paternal grandmother, then, clockwise around the table: my elder sister, Ding; my mother; me; Third Brother; my father; Qingzeng; Shaozeng; my big brother's wife; Yunqin; and my big brother. The dishes always included chicken, duck, fish, pork, and my particular favorite, cassava meatballs.

They were simple to make: cassava flour was combined with minced pork, and the mixture was seasoned and formed into meatballs about the size of fortune cookies. These were slightly flattened and placed in a steamer basket to be cooked. Then the basket was brought to the table.

They were tasty and chewy, and not at all fatty. I thought they were delicious. Every year, when the adults had long since left the table and gone off somewhere to chat, we youngsters remained to fight over the food. The cooked meatballs were very sticky, and had to be pried off the base of the steamer basket, not easy with chopsticks. Ding was quick-witted and quick-fingered: no sooner had she picked one out than it was in her mouth. But on one occasion, something odd happened: she fastened her chopsticks around a meatball and went to raise it to her lips but it wouldn't budge. She gave a tug, we heard a *ping,* and one chopstick snapped in two. She had inadvertently pushed it through a hole in the steamer, which proved stronger than the chopsticks. This was seventy-eight years ago and I have never forgotten it! Time flies but some things stick in the memory. There was nothing for it but to wait for another basket to be brought.

虎皮鸭子

南城古风尚存，食品原料简朴，烧制时也并不复杂。所谓"虎皮鸭子"者，係用粉皮作外层，内层铺以薯粉蒸熟後切成条状物，再加些调料如豆豉之類烧煮而成。但吃时别有风味，毫无油腻之感，素食者多喜食之，此菜可以上酒席，其品位可以想见矣。

薯粉肉丸

原料非常简单，用猪肉末加上薯粉揉捏成小圆球状，再压扁，上蒸笼蒸熟，趁热吃，味道又鲜又糯，有嚼劲。我家平常不吃，只在吃年夜饭时才做。等于是菜後的点心。有一年，吃了一笼又一笼，大家争着吃。由于此物有粘性，用筷子汤用力箝才能到喷定姐的筷子插到蒸笼的竹格子中间，她未发觉，用力一提，把筷子都弄断了一根。

OPPOSITE

Tiger skin duck

TOP RIGHT Nancheng county still retained the old ways of eating: simple ingredients, simply cooked. What we called "tiger skin duck" was a wrap made of a starch skin, filled with sweet potato noodles. This was steamed, flavored with condiments such as black beans, rolled up, and then fried. The rolls were quite distinctive, not oily at all, and were a favorite snack for vegetarians (since they had no actual duck in them). They were so good that they were often served at banquets.

Cassava meatballs

BOTTOM LEFT

Many years later, in Shanghai, Meitang and I were talking about cassava meatballs. She enjoyed her food, and so we bought all the raw ingredients and got to work making our own. They were a disappointment. Perhaps we were not sufficiently proficient in the culinary arts. In any event, the balls we produced were nothing compared to the ones our cook used to serve.

Normally we children were forbidden to play cards or dominoes, but New Year was different. Not only were we permitted to play *paijiu,* but we had Father to act as banker, which was thrilling. Once we had finished our New Year's Eve meal, Ding called the servants to clear the dishes, and when the table was ready, she went to the study to call Father: "Ready! Ready! Come and play *paijiu*!" And Father would emerge, grinning. As the banker, he sat at the head of the table.

Everyone gathered around, the family of my big brother and my sister-in-law, and my grandmother too, on his right; Ding was in charge of their dominoes. My mother, my younger brother Shouru, and I sat on the banker's left, and I was in charge of our dominoes. My father brought out twenty silver dollars, changed them for the equivalent in small tokens, and put them on the table in front of him. It looked like an enormous pile of money. Shouru and I partnered up; we each put the two dollars from our New Year's gifts into a tube-shaped cigarette tin. In order to bring us luck, I wrote the words "money-earning tube" on it in big characters.

欢乐的除夕之夜

A joyful New Year's Eve

Among those present were Big Brother, Sister-in-Law, Grandmother, Father, Shouru, Pingru, Uncle Yu Zhong, Second Sister (Ding), Old Ao

故乡南城民众过年时必备之菜
—— "小炒" 和 "骨子"

Popular Nancheng New Year dishes

LEFT Small fries RIGHT "Bones."

All the staff crowded around to see the fun: my father's secretary (Yu Zhongyang, or Uncle Yu Zhong as we called him), our chef, our rickshaw puller, the three women servants, and the wet nurse that my sister-in-law employed. They positioned themselves behind the people they reckoned were most reliable, and placed small bets to see if they would get lucky. My sister Ding was so quick that all the servants believed she would win, and she always had the most people behind her. The best moments during our *paijiu* games were when the banker paid out. Amid gales of laughter, my father would smile and push the dominoes away and begin to count out the money owed.

Sometimes there would be an unclaimed bet. Then there would be frantic shouts and old Mrs. Li would come rushing in, saying she had placed it but had just gone to her room to attend to some little thing. Now she was as thrilled as if she was "outside the Sword Gate, suddenly hearing of the taking of Jibei," as the Du Fu poem puts it.[4]

By this point all the electric lights were on, and the main gate was firmly shut for the night. Everyone's attention was fixed on my father as he again piled up the thirty-two dominoes in front of him, then threw the dice and counted up the scores. We could not help counting along with him. But sometimes the rolling dice teased us, pirouetting on one edge like a ballet dancer, round and round the table. Silence fell and everyone held their breath until finally, through sheer force of gravity, the little dice could turn no more and dropped on the tabletop, and the number was revealed.

Father always lost: when he won, he carried on playing, and so his winnings were whittled away until they were all gone and he would admit defeat. If he had lost everything and it was still early, he would get out another ten or twenty dollars, and continue until he was routed once more. I never paid much attention to who won. All I knew was that my "money-earning tube" was always on the losing side.

For the first few days of the New Year, we had vegetarian food. It came in big dishes and there was plenty of it. There was one dish called "small fries," which consisted of bamboo shoots sliced thin as matchsticks, stir-fried with dried bean-curd skins. There was another dish called "bones," which actually had nothing to do with meat bones but was dried bean curd cut into cubes and fried with cubed bamboo shoots. On New Year's Day itself, we never ate meat in our family. Not because we wanted to lose weight but because if you ate vegetarian food on the first day of the year, it symbolized being vegetarian for the whole year.

母亲和我们一起扎狮子灯

My mother made the lion lantern with us.

On the morning of New Year's Day, the whole family made offerings to the ancestors. We lined up in procession, with Father leading the way, followed by my big brother, me, Third Brother, Qingzeng, and the others, everyone holding a stick of incense, starting from the great hall, at the rear of the complex, and proceeding right to the main gate, bowing to one side and the other, our hands clasped together. It was called "journeying." Then we stuck our incense sticks into the dirt outside the main gate at the street edge and at the corners of the wall. Men were always leaving home, and this journeying ceremony was to pay our respects to the spirits around us, and ask their protection for our journeys.

In later years, I joined the army and traveled all over the country. I was destined not to return to my birthplace for many decades, and by that time it had long since been razed to the ground. Occasionally, I would recall those New Year's incense sticks, and the wisps of smoke rising from them to dissipate in the air of those tranquil times. They brought with them fond memories of my family back then.

At the Lantern Festival of 1938, I decided that I would make a lion lantern and join the lantern procession myself. In Nancheng county, the Lantern Festival celebrations began on the thirteenth day of the first lunar month. Peasants flocked into the county town with their dragon lanterns, parading from house to house to the accompaniment of drums, cymbals, and dancing. The townsfolk set off firecrackers at their courtyard gates, to "welcome the lanterns." As the firecrackers exploded, the dragon lanterns would leap into their dances, to be rewarded with red envelopes of money after they finished.

母亲替我剪兰花

My mother cut out an orchid for me.

Text on cutout reads: "The perfume of emperors."

OPPOSITE

TOP LEFT My paternal grandfather, Rao Zhixiang (his courtesy name was Fujiu[5]), 1864–1912. He was from Nancheng county. In Year 20 of the reign of Guangxu (1894), he passed the highest imperial civil service examination with flying colors and became a compiler and editor at Hanlin Academy. He also acted as the imperial supervising censor for Sichuan province and was appointed as chief examiner for Hubei province, although he did not take up his post there. He passed away at the age of forty-nine. I never met him, but as a child I saw his portrait when we made sacrifices to the ancestors and have re-created it from memory.

BOTTOM RIGHT My father's mother was a Zhang and also hailed from Nancheng. She lived to the age of seventy-three. In those days, titles would be conferred on the wives of successful candidates. My grandfather was a grade-three official, so my grandmother was given the title Virtuous Woman. (The wives of first-grade officials were given the title Lady, the wives of fifth-grade officials were titled Respected, the wives of seventh-grade officials were titled Mother.) The robe she wears was given to her by the Imperial Court and was something she treasured for the rest of her life. At court celebrations, the wives of officials of grade five and above were invited along with their husbands and were required to wear their court robes. I saw my grandmother in this robe only once, and that was in Nanchang city when my father held a sixtieth birthday party for her. This was a grand feast, and the room was lit by an array of gas lamps. My grandmother put on her phoenix headdress and robe and posed for photographs with the whole family. Her robe was dark blue, richly embroidered with silver thread. I touched it with curiosity—it was thick and heavy. It was a great honor for her to wear it, but it cannot have been very comfortable.

祖父饒芝祥，字符九，江西南城人（一八六四～一九一二）。光緒三十年（一九○四）中二甲第三名進士，點翰林，官翰林院編修、四川道監察御史、湖北省主考（未赴任）。享年四十九歲。我沒有見過他，此像是我根據幼年祭祖時所看到他的遺容重新回憶而畫的。

祖母張氏，江西南城人，享年七十三歲。科舉時代講究的是「夫榮妻貴」，「封妻蔭子」。由於我祖父官居三品，所以她被朝廷封為淑人（一品稱「夫人」；二、三品稱「淑人」；四、五品稱「恭人」；六、七品稱孺人）。這身「朝服」乃朝廷所賜，也是她畢生引以為榮的「珍寶」。朝廷中遇有喜慶事或慶典一般名集五品以上官員帶著眷屬前往宮中慶賀賜宴，都必須穿著朝服。我只看見過一次祖母穿這件衣服，那是在南昌父親為她舉辦六十壽誕、大宴賓客懸燈（洋燈）結彩，她頭戴鳳冠，身穿朝服，與我們全家拍照。她的朝服為深藍色綉有金銀線的各種花紋圖案，我好奇地摸了摸，又厚又重，穿上去僅有莊嚴肅穆之感但未必舒服。

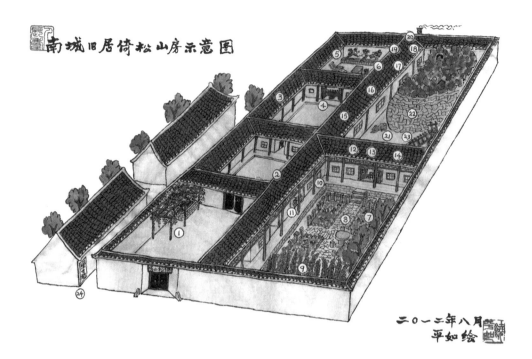

Sketch of the layout of Yi Song Shan Fang, our old home in Nancheng county.

1. The grapevine frames. 2. Grandmother's bedroom. 3. My father's sister's house. 4. Ancestral hall. 5. Father's sitting room. 6. Father's study. 7. Garden. 8. Stone table and benches. 9. Hibiscus (when its flowers had been dried, they could be fried and eaten, and they were a particular favorite of my grandmother. I liked to mix these sweet-smelling flowers into my rice porridge). 10. The room where I practiced my calligraphy. 11. Lobby where we kept our bicycles. 12. Mother's bedroom. 13. Living room. 14. The room where Father received visitors. 15. Library. 16. The bedroom and study I shared with Third Brother. 17. Buddhist shrine. 18. Dining room. 19. Father's second study. 20. Kitchen. 21. Our dog, Humor (when we fled the fighting and took refuge in Guangchang county, Fuzhou district, Jiangxi province, Humor was left behind to guard the house. When Japanese troops broke into our home, he barked furiously at them and they shot him dead). 22. Air-raid shelter (to protect us from Japanese aerial bombardment, we built our own shelter, with bamboo slats for the outer walls, a roof of earth, and benches inside). 23. Pedal-operated water pump (we had no plumbing inside the shelter, so the water had to be pumped out manually). 24. Alley beyond the wall, originally nameless but later called Scholar's Alley, because my grandfather had been engaged in compilation work for Hanlin Academy.

That year, I bought lengths of bamboo and split them into thin strips. Then I purchased thin wire and colored paper. After that, it was up to my imagination, as I wove the strips into the shape of a lion's head and body, supported by thicker pieces of bamboo inside, which allowed me to manipulate my lion. For the lion's eyes, I used the bulbs from two torches, fixing the battery to a stick inside the head and making a circuit with copper wires. The person manipulating the lion's head had to hold it up with one hand while with the other he had to make the contact between the wires, so that the eyes appeared to flash. In those days, this was a singularly creative lighting effect. For the exterior of the lion lantern, I first covered it with a layer of white paper, then attached the lion's fur, thin strips of green paper. I pasted on layer after layer of these strips, working on it from early morning till five o'clock in the afternoon. There were a few other boys in the family that I tried to co-opt: Third Brother; my big brother's son Qingzeng; my sister's son Rongzi; and a cousin, Xili, but they were too young to be of much use. Evening approached and nearly half the lion's fur remained to be stuck on. Just as I began to despair, my mother came to call us to dinner, took in the situation, and decided to help. She had nimble fingers and often helped me out in a crisis.

I still remember that when I was in fourth grade of primary school, we were told to make something with our hands for homework. I forgot to do it, and it had to be turned in that afternoon. I was in a panic. My mother got some red paper and, without even sketching a design, simply took a pair of scissors and began snipping away. In no time at all, an orchid had appeared. "Orchids are the perfume of emperors," she told me. "You inscribe the words 'the perfume of emperors.'" And now, as my mother lent a hand, my lion too was completed.

By the time I had shoveled down some dinner, it was nearly six o'clock. I quickly divided the tasks: Shouru would hold up the lion's head—he was bright and nimble so he could handle the responsibility. Cousin Xili, who was about the same age as Shouru, and the same size, would hold up the lion's body. Qingzeng and Rongzi each held a bamboo lath that had been split down the middle for half its length, and walked in front to clear the way, swishing and cracking the laths in the air. My role was to conceal myself in the crowds as our lion lantern went by and applaud loudly.

日机轰炸南昌

Japanese planes bombed Nanchang city.

At seven o'clock it was quite dark, a fine, clear night. The shops on either side of West Street were all festooned with colored lanterns. The streets were packed with people, with only a narrow space down the middle for the lantern parade to pass through. The sounds of drums and gongs and firecrackers drew nearer, and, one by one, the troupes came into view. I stood squeezed in among the crowds, peering at the dragon lanterns, the horse lanterns, the lotus lanterns, and the flower drum lanterns as they went by. Finally, that year's one and only lion lantern arrived. Qingzeng and Rongzi cleared the way, brandishing their bamboo sticks, and behind them the lion's eyes sparkled most amusingly. Thanks to Third Brother, it all went without a hitch.

I followed along behind them. As we turned in to North Street, the lights and the crowds thinned out. So we picked a couple of larger stores and went in to perform, shouting New Year good wishes. It was customary for the shopkeepers to reward the lantern dancers, but after a few performances, we had garnered only four or five pairs of small candles and not a cent in actual money. My capital outlay on materials—the bamboo, the wire, the paper, and the batteries—amounted to several silver dollars, so I was seriously out of pocket.

That year, a big dragon lantern turned up at our home. The troupe consisted of a dozen or so people, banging gongs and drums and dancing. The dragon lantern whirled around the hall, firecrackers exploded, and the room filled with smoke. The candlelight flickered, and the candle shadows wavered against the wall. I felt intoxicated by the splendid display, and the attendant whiff of gunpowder, but I was also aware that all good things had to come to an end, and the final curtain would eventually come down on these New Year festivities. We cheered the performance, red envelopes were given out, and the dragon lantern jubilantly rushed away to another house.

When I was eight, the family moved to the provincial capital, Nanchang city. Then when I was sixteen, the War Against Japan broke out, and Japanese planes bombarded the city. We had to leave. We moved back to Nancheng county, and I continued my studies at Xin Yuan Middle School.

Rao Zhixiang had purchased our house, Yi Song Shan Fang (House on Pine Mountain). I never met him, but I had been in his study, and my father often told me how, as a child, he had had to spend many arduous hours at his lessons. On the walls of the study hung a scroll of calligraphy executed in a bold and flamboyant hand. I could not make out what it meant, except that it was signed by the Song dynasty poet, painter, and calligrapher Mi Fu.[6] The thin silk had gone as dark as soy sauce with age. I still find this "curing" process that occurs with old silk profoundly moving.

Every summer, my father would bring the books and scrolls out of his study and give them an airing, handling them with the utmost care and reverence. When we moved to Nanchang city, there was much we had to leave behind, but my father was anxious about these Song and Yuan dynasty texts and brought them with us. Every year, when the sun was at its hottest, trestle tables would be set up in an inner courtyard and the books and rubbings would be laid out on them. All we children knew about them was that books were among the good things of this world. The rubbings were sizable; they went on and on unrolling, all white letters on a black background. The large script of the general Yue Fei was revealed in the bright sunlight, with his famous words "Restore our lost land."[7]

Nancheng had two ancient bridges, Ten Thousand Years Bridge and Peace Bridge. Our house was quite near the latter. Peace Bridge was at its best at sundown in summertime—as dusk fell, a cooling breeze over the river picked up, and I used to go with three or four school friends to lean over the parapet at East Gate, near the bridgehead, to chat and sing songs. My grandfather had written a song to celebrate the charm of the place:

Beneath the bridge, wavelets crest,
The sun has not yet retreated behind the Dafu Mountains
The last wisp of evening mist sinks into the trees,
The sky clears, pinpricks of light from fishing boats appear on the river island.

One day when I was sixteen, I was at Peace Bridge enjoying the breeze as usual when I looked up and saw the evening light change all of a sudden: over the lofty Gu Mountains there was a spectacular crimson sky. I looked down at the sharp angle of the bridge pier at my feet—to me it looked just like the sharpened prow of a paddle steamer—where the current, bringing with it bits of vegetation from upstream, was cleft in two and swirled into eddies and whirlpools that finally dissolved as the waters flowed on down. I lapsed into a daze, assailed by thoughts about this human world in the encroaching gloom. Of course, they were nothing more than juvenile musings, yet I still remember that day.

Many decades sped by, and one day, in midsummer of 2008, I went back to Nancheng county and revisited Peace Bridge. The wooden parapet I used to lean against, like the bridge itself, had been replaced by a concrete structure. A tall teahouse stood where the bridgehead, the East Gate, and the city wall used to be. The buildings of the old days, the busy crowds of shopkeepers and people carrying their burdens on shoulder poles or on their backs, or pushing carts—these were all gone. But when I raised my eyes, I saw the exact same shape of the Gu Mountains that had made such an impression on me as a boy. And when I looked down, the bridge pier still looked just the same. The waters of the Xu River still rolled under the bridge, were cleft in two by the pier and drawn into whirlpools, then surged on downstream in a great rush of water. All of a sudden, I felt at peace. The moonlight, the mountains, the waters were the same tranquil presence as ever, and the Milky Way still sparkled overhead. It was as if they were intent on pointing up the contrast with the impermanence of human existence.

MEITANG

Meitang and I did know of each other as children, because our families were old friends, but we met on only two occasions. Those moments could have become treasured memories,[8] but regrettably we were both happily absorbed in our own young lives in those days. (I heard the stories that follow much later, when she herself told me about her life as a young girl.)

The first time we met was soon after Meitang and her family had arrived in the French Concession in Hankou[9] and they went to visit relatives in the county of Nancheng. On their way back to Hankou, they dropped in on us in Nanchang city. I remember getting out one of my toys and showing her how it worked. She was ten years old.

After we moved back to Nanchang county from Nanchang city, she and her family came again, this time for dinner. However, I had eaten early and was in a hurry to be off to the Xie Clan Memorial Hall, five li (about one and a half miles) away. That was in the countryside in those days, and the hall was pleasantly cool. I used to go there with a few good friends from school to spend the night and escape the summer heat. There were no lights on the country roads, and we took torches for the half-hour walk. Just as I was leaving, I passed by the room where the family was eating and saw Meitang. She was still a child, and a small, slight one at that, so someone had put a stool on top of the chair, to raise her up so she could reach the table.

Sometime later, Meitang told me that she remembered seeing me then too: "You had a torch and you were flashing it on and off." She was thirteen.

我拿出新买的玩具给美棠玩

I brought out a new toy to show Meitang.

我的新玩具

My new toy: exterior (top) and interior (bottom)

I asked Meitang if she had any idea then that she and I would get engaged and then marry. She said she remembered her older cousin Mao Yisun telling her that very day: "You should marry Pingru! He's good-looking, he's got lovely eyes!"

Meitang's grandfather had built up a Chinese medicine business from scratch and ran a shop called Mao Fuchun's Chinese Pharmacy. He then purchased land and a house in Nancheng county and got to know my grandfather.

Meitang's father took over the business. He was a prudent businessman who worked hard and subsequently opened a second shop. He worked mainly in Fujian province and in Hankou city, and it was in Hankou that Meitang spent most of her childhood.

制鹿茸粉之圖

二〇〇八、七、廿八、平

请工人到家中制鹿茸

A worker was brought in to grind the deer antler into powder.

It was because of the family's Chinese medicine business that Meitang fell seriously ill on one occasion. She had never been strong, and the summer when she was five years old, her mother dosed her with deer antler. She had no knowledge of Chinese medicine, except that she had heard that deer antler was a powerful health supplement. She had no idea that it created "dry heat" and should be given to the frail and elderly only in very small quantities. It was certainly not suitable for a child like Meitang. Soon after she took it, her nose began to bleed, and she developed a burning fever and lost consciousness.

The doctor was called, and he immediately laid Meitang on the ground. He sent for river sludge, plastered it on cloths, covered her all over, and gave her medicine to "clear the heat." Some days later, Meitang finally regained consciousness.

美棠误服麛茸进行抢救

Meitang gets emergency treatment for an overdose of deer antler.

Another time, her mother made bird's nest soup and gave it to the maidservant to take to her. Meitang took a sip, decided it was tasteless, and poured the rest straight into the spittoon. The maidservant went to tell the mother, who rushed in and slapped Meitang, exclaiming, "I spent all day preparing this for you!"

Meitang didn't like fatty meat or vegetables. What she really wanted to eat, just like all kids, was deep-fried and crispy food. In fact, she refused to eat anything except that, and her mother had to go along with it, and serve her deep-fried fish and sautéed meat at every meal. She had to examine slices of sausage in bright sunlight and extract every scrap of fat, and fresh vegetables never made an appearance at the table. Eventually, too much "internal heat" built up, and Meitang got a bad sore throat and, more seriously, a chest infection. Luckily, by this time her mother had become a bit more enlightened and took her to a foreigners' hospital in Hankou, where she quickly recovered. However, even when she was eighty-four and was admitted to Shanghai East China Hospital with kidney failure, the doctors could still see the lesions from her childhood illness on her X-rays.

Meitang had an older sister named Yutang, who was mute as the result of an overdose of powdered pearl given to her as a child when she had a serious throat infection. Her parents sent her to a school for the deaf and dumb, where she learned sign language. She was an unhappy girl, and, when not in school, stayed home all the time. She never showed herself to visitors and was rather jealous of Meitang. Meitang should have felt sorry for her, but she was too young to understand. The sisters fought constantly. They shared a bed, and Yutang drew a "demarcation line" down the middle of the sheet every night, which she would not allow Meitang to cross. Meitang gave as good as she got. Each sister had a metal box for her pocket money, which she kept by her pillow, and after Yutang had gone to school, Meitang secretly used to open her sister's to count how much was inside. If it was less than her own, then she did not mind. But if it was more, she nagged her parents until they brought hers up to the same amount.

"Meitang sneaked off again!"

Every time Meitang sneaked out to play, Yutang would tell their parents: she held her right hand, palm downward, at waist level to indicate her "little sister," then pointed with her left forefinger out the door to indicate that she had "sneaked off again!"

"A young gentleman has ways and means to get money," as the old saying goes. But what was a young lady to do? Meitang stole from her father, she admitted to me—she liked a bit of excitement. On occasion, she crept from her bed in the dead of night and tiptoed barefoot to her parents' room. She knew where her father hung his clothes and slipped his key to the safe from his pocket. She was familiar with the safe and opened it without difficulty. She did not dare touch the big money, but she grabbed a few coins from the stack of silver and put them in her pocket. Then she quickly shut the safe, returned the key, retreated to her room, and went back to sleep.

美棠幼时夜间"偷"钱图

Meitang stealing money as a child

But she did not know that the safe had to be locked with the key. The next morning, her father would exclaim to her mother: "How can I have been so careless, I must have forgotten to lock the safe yesterday evening, how extraordinary!" And Meitang would hug herself in secret glee.

At New Year, her father used to give Meitang and her sister ten silver dollars each. But Meitang did not let him off that easily and demanded more. Her father was forced to placate her secretly with an extra ten dollars. For the first three days of the New Year, it was usual for the house to be thronged with her father's business associates coming to pay their respects. Meitang was under orders to play in her room and not come out.

But she was a strong-willed child. She used to peer through the crack in the door, and, as soon as the guests arrived, she would rush out and wish them a happy New Year. The guests, aware that Mr. Mao had a favorite daughter, would come prepared, and Meitang received New Year money from each of them: at least two yuan, and sometimes as much as ten. I did the math and worked out that she must have raked in a good deal of money every New Year.

In the alley outside Meitang's family home was a fruit store, with an owner who knew all the gossip about the local families. Meitang passed by every day and helped herself to any bits of fruit that took her fancy. The owner duly chalked it up to her account and, at the end of each month, presented the bill to her father.

2009.9.16.秉如 [印]

This was the normal way to do business with long-standing customers in those days. So actually Meitang had nothing on which to spend the bits of money she had taken so much trouble to accumulate. Still, it was a great game to save up more than her sister, and she enjoyed it thoroughly.

Meitang went to the Fu Ren Primary School in Hankou, which was run by Christian missionaries. Her parents were not eager for her to make the journey alone, so they hired a maid who was five years older than she was to go with her. As Meitang sat in her lessons, she used to see the maid in the school playground, playing happily on the swings or the slide. It made her terribly envious, but she just had to put up with it. After class, the two girls went home together.

Meitang was a clever and competitive child, but she only ever came second in exams. There was another girl in the class, a Miss Fu, two years older than Meitang and an incredibly hard worker. Meitang never managed to oust her from first place, a situation on which she brooded unhappily. Years later, when she told me about it, she still looked aggrieved.

TEXT ACCOMPANYING THE ILLUSTRATION

Meitang told me the maid's name, but unfortunately I cannot remember it now. The maid was brave and quick-witted. On the way home, they were sometimes accosted by gangs of children intent on bullying Meitang, and on each occasion, the maid fought back, and the young scoundrels soon fled.

One day when Meitang was ten, she was playing in her father's store, and the book-keeper, who was busy addressing parcels, asked: "Can you write?" "Yes!" "Can you address these parcels nicely for me?" "Yes!" Meitang perched on a small stool placed on top of another and began to write the address on each parcel under the fascinated gaze of the customers. There was so much loud praise for her efforts that her proud father agreed she should continue her studies.

Text on red banner: "Ten thousand ounces of gold." In those days, it was common for businesses to have auspicious phrases hung around the shop. "Ten thousand ounces of gold" is one such phrase. In fact, when written vertically, it contains overlapping elements and the four characters merge into two.

2009. 9. 16.

On the school playground, there was a track made of colored bricks, with footprints marked in a contrasting color, showing how to walk gracefully. Meitang used to practice on it every day after class, so that when she grew up she could be a graceful young lady.

After the outbreak of the War Against Japan, the Fu Ren Primary School moved to the interior of China, taking some of the pupils. Meitang's father, loath to do business with the Japanese and their Chinese collaborators, shut his stores and his bank, and moved his family to the French Concession in Hankou. Meitang continued her education in a privately run school there.

In the new school, Meitang made a best friend, a girl called Liu Baozhen. Baozhen's father was a skilled musician who played the *qin* for the famous Peking opera singer Mei Lanfang, so the family was very well off even though they were not in commerce. Mr. Liu had taken Baozhen's younger sister Baozhu to live in Hong Kong, leaving Baozhen with her mother in Hankou. The mother was both unconventional and enterprising: she managed a hotel called the Railway Hotel, and opened a dance hall and a department store called the Yun Chang Company.

Inside Meitang's family's house there was a screen, so that even if people strayed in, they could not see what was going on in the house. The character 福, for "good fortune," was pasted on the inward-facing side of the screen. Outside those walls, the fires of war raged so fiercely that even the most stoutly defended house was unlikely to hold out for long. But Meitang's father went to great pains to protect the eight members of his family.

日机轰炸汉口市区

2009.9.17 平如

抗日战争爆发

一九三七年七月七日日本军国主义者悍然发动七·七卢沟桥事变，爆发了全面的侵华战争。战火不久就燃烧到汉口，日机在汉口狂轰滥炸，汉口随即沦入日寇魔掌。岳父是个爱国正直的商人，不愿与敌伪、汉奸集乃将做生意的商栈、钱庄关门歇业，携着一家先小搬入汉口的法租界，因此处感比较安全些。

初系向不临川人租一幢房屋，此人集贩卖毒致富，是个暴发户，为人刻薄寡高，经常来屋观察，说这里弄坏了，那里又弄坏了……岳父气极及便不住他家的房子。干脆自己设计，建造一幢两层楼房，外面用红砖砌的围墙特别高，故光线通风都不佳，大门特别厚铁锁特别粗，其将点就是谨慎与安全。右图另岳父去法租界所建房屋的示意图。在兵荒马乱之际家中又无北年男子为了家中妇孺姐妈安全，此乃岳父当年之苦衷也，不能有半点疏忽。

岳父去法租界自建住宅示意图

2009.9.24. 平如

法租界里的生活

辅仁小学此时已迁往内地，有些学生随校迁，美棠乃转入租界内一个私立学校就读。嵒父母家人口已增至8人，再加上女佣、奶妈等生活费担日渐加重。

当时租界内生活费用昂贵，一担水要三夫大洋二元。租界当局每日规定时间可用大龙头免费供水，但需要排队接水。美棠便叫岳父去买几只水桶，排着水桶排队。女佣人则隔些时候拎前去观察，列差不多的时候，女佣便

把盛满水的水桶拎回家。美棠年纪虽小却已懂得如何设法为家庭节省开支，来度过难关了。

2009.9.18 平如

▲ 美棠排队接水图

Outbreak of the War Against Japan

The city of Hankou under Japanese aerial bombardment

TOP LEFT, PAGE 64 On July 7, 1937, the Japanese imperialists launched an unprovoked attack on Chinese troops outside Beijing. This, the so-called Marco Polo Bridge Incident, launched Japan's war of aggression against the whole of China.[10] The war soon engulfed Hankou, which fell into enemy hands after Japanese planes pounded it from the air. My future father-in-law was an honest man who loved his country and had no wish to do business with either the Japanese enemy or their Chinese collaborators. He shut up shop and moved his entire family into the French Concession in the belief that they would be safer there.

Sketch of the house my father-in-law built in the French Concession

BOTTOM RIGHT, PAGE 64 At first they rented a house from a compatriot from Linchuan, a nouveau-riche who had made his money in the narcotics trade. He was a tightfisted landlord, constantly dropping in to keep an eye on things and picking on some imagined bit of damage to his property. Meitang's father got so angry that he designed and built his own two-story house. This had a very high red-brick surrounding wall, which unfortunately kept both the light and the breeze out; the entrance gate was very thick and secured with stout chains. This picture is my father-in-law's plan for the new house. In those tumultuous times, great care had to be taken to protect the women and children at home, as there were no able-bodied men on hand. Nothing could be overlooked. It all caused Mr. Mao a great deal of heartache.

Life in the French Concession

BOTTOM LEFT PAGE 65 The Fu Ren Primary School moved to the interior of China, taking some of the students with it, but Meitang stayed in Hankou, attending classes in a privately run school in the French Concession. The household now consisted of eight people, not counting the maids, nanny, and so on, and it became ever harder to keep everyone fed and clothed.

The cost of living in the concession was astronomical—a couple of buckets of water carried on a shoulder pole cost two silver dollars. The concession authorities had decreed free use of public standpipes at a certain time each day, but the queues were immensely long. Meitang asked her father to buy some big buckets and went to stand in line herself. She got a maidservant to keep an eye on the progress of the queue and then, when her turn came and she had filled her buckets with water herself, to carry the full buckets home for her.

By age fourteen or fifteen, Meitang and Baozhen were old enough to go out and enjoy themselves. They spent a lot of time at the family's dance hall and became accomplished ballroom dancers. Together they strolled in the park, went window shopping, ate out, and saw films. They bought identical outfits—clothes, socks, and shoes—had their hair permed in the same style and their photographs taken together. Baozhen married into the Xiao family but continued to invite Meitang to visit her. In time, Baozhen's fourth brother-in-law took a great fancy to Meitang. His mother regarded her as a charming,

2009.9.25. 平如

舞起中池舞在一女少个兩珍宝与棠美 ▲

intelligent girl and did her best to bring the pair together, finding excuses to get her over to help with simple sewing and embroidery. Fortunately, Meitang had no interest in the boy, and her parents did not want her to marry into a family from another province.

Meitang's family spent all the war years, from 1937 to 1945, in the French Concession, where they were increasingly impoverished. So after the Japanese were defeated, her father threw himself into running his Hankou businesses once more, and sent his wife and children to their house in Linchuan. They hired a boat to transport themselves and some household effects. On the eve of their departure, Baozhen's mother was eager for Meitang to come to dinner. "Will you be coming back to Hankou?" she asked. "Perhaps," said Meitang. Early next morning, Baozhen came alone to the riverbank and stood waving goodbye to Meitang. The two girls had been inseparable for eight years. Meitang watched as the boat drew farther away and the shoreline faded from view. The last thing she saw was the figure of Baozhen, still standing there.

That year, Meitang was almost twenty. When her father sent his earnings back to the family in Linchuan, she took charge of the household spending.

A riverside farewell

Amid the barrage of gunfire, I told myself that
I was probably going to die and be buried right there.

2
I Go to War

The day the Japs invade, the scholar casts his pen aside.
If a home is destroyed to save a country from ruin, that is our bounden duty.
Officials and generals are made, not born. They will destroy the enemy and
*   return in triumph.*
Success achieved, our son will return to the bosom of the family, and reverence
*   his elders.*

—A poem my father wrote for me, just before I left

A bright moon hangs amid fleeting clouds. The country must be protected with
*   sincerity, ambition, and determination.*
Our eldest son must not worry about us, just send a letter to say that he is safe.

—A poem my mother wrote for me, just before I left

I burn at the injustice of our shattered land, there is weeping and wailing
*   throughout the Southeast.*
A bright sword tip sharpened for ten years, with such great goals, why should
*   I be anxious about not achieving them?*

—A poem I wrote myself

In 1940 the War Against Japan had entered its third year. In my second year at Xin Yuan Middle School, I was eighteen years old and becoming aware of the terrible troubles facing my country and its people. In July, the First Command, Central Military (Whampoa) Academy was recruiting for its Term 18 intake in Shangrao city.[11] Having finally got my parents' permission, I set off with three school friends to take the entrance exams.

OPPOSITE

TOP LEFT When we four got to Shangrao, we lodged at Dechangyi, an old Chinese medicine establishment. The owner, Jiang Jiayu, was a relative of one of my friends. He was extremely welcoming and treated us like his own family. We lived and ate at the shop for a whole month while we registered for the exams and subsequently reported. I have never forgotten his hospitality.

IN CIRCLE The exams took two days: first came a fairly basic physical examination—we were measured and weighed; our sight, hearing, and so on were checked; and our pulses were taken, but our blood pressure was not, and there were no blood tests. However, there was one very important test: for color blindness. This was

我们4人来到上饶，住在当地一家著名的中药店里。店名"德长怡"店主江家瑜老伯是D君的亲戚。他待我们亲如子侄，非常热情关怀备至，食宿都在店中，时间长达一个月（包括报考以及后来报到等），此情至今难以忘怀。

军校考试为期2天。第一天体格检查，很简单：量身高体重，听心跳，看看五官；没有量血压和验血这一套。但当时有一项检查是很重要的，即：检查色盲，方法是：给你看几页由许多淡色彩的小圆点所组成的画面，其中"藏"有数字图形，你如能正确读出数字，便说明你没有色盲。有色盲的人不能录取。

检查有无色盲的
画面

第二天笔试，在一间厅堂里举行。上午国文，下午数学，题目不难。中午，每人还发两个肉包子作为午餐。我当时觉得相当满意。

how it was done: you were given several pictures composed of dots in pale colors, with numerals concealed among them. If you correctly identified the numerals, that meant you did not have color blindness. The color-blind were not eligible to enroll.

BOTTOM RIGHT The second day we took a written test: Chinese language in the morning and mathematics in the afternoon, neither of them very difficult. Lunch was two meat buns each, which I found very satisfactory.

BOTTOM LEFT The color blindness test

过了个把月,我在家门口收到了军校的"录取通知书",我非常高兴。同时得知:D君和L君也被录取了;只有R君由于眼睛欠佳而"名落孙山"。

我积极作出发前的准备工作,在裁缝店定做了一个相当大的、绿色帆布的"童子军"式背包;买了200张明信片以便随时给家中发信;还买了手电筒、防风眼镜以及一些必需日用品。母亲给我准备了羊毛毡和随身衣服。父亲给我200元钱作为旅途中费用。我还特意在背包的另一面用白布设计制作了四个美术字——"长征万里",表示好男儿应该有"乘长风破万里浪"的豪迈气概,奔赴抗日救国的征程。

A month later, the postman delivered my Military Academy admission papers to the door. I was very happy. I found out that two of my friends had also been admitted; the third had failed the medical exam due to poor eyesight.

Full of enthusiasm, I made my preparations. First I went to the tailor and ordered a sizable green canvas cadet's knapsack. I bought two hundred postcards, so that I could stay in touch with the family. I bought a flashlight and wind goggles, and a few other necessities. My mother gave me a woolen blanket and clothes, and my father gave me two hundred yuan as traveling money. I also wrote and cut out the calligraphic characters for "Ten-Thousand-Li-Long March" in white cloth and attached them on the side of the knapsack against my back. These mettlesome words were to show that a real man "braves the winds and the waves," as the poet put it.

Text on knapsack: "Ten-Thousand-Li-Long March"

Just as we were about to leave, one of my friends gave in to his family's pleas and dropped out. That left two of us. We got a lift in an army truck loaded with boxes of ammunition and headed for Yingtan city. The driver had been drinking and was reprimanded at an army checkpoint en route. This made him so angry that he drove even more erratically until, when we were still thirty li from Yingtan, the truck overturned. It landed on its right side. I happened to be sitting on the left side, with my friend on the right. As it went over, he was pinned underneath a pile of ammo cases and sustained some nasty injuries. I landed on top and escaped with cuts and scrapes. My friend was greatly upset by this misadventure, and when we reached Shangrao, he decided to drop out too. I was the only one to present myself at the enrollment office of the Military Academy.

起上饶报到时,在距鹰潭还
有30里的地方翻车

On the way to Shangrao city to enroll, the
truck overturned when we were thirty li
from Yingtan.

报到后,在上饶市区外的一个大祠堂里集中

After enrollment, we all gathered at a large clan memorial hall on the outskirts of Shangrao city.

In Shangrao, we waited for another couple of weeks for new recruits from Jinhua city (Zhejiang province) and Tunxi city (Anhui province) to join us. We were billeted in a large clan memorial hall on the outskirts of the city. In front of the hall was an area of beaten earth where we were served our meals, and we used a stream that trickled past for washing. But most of the time we spent strolling around the streets, eating, drinking, and amusing ourselves, so we were hardly ever there to eat the bland, communal meals.

Toward the end of September, our cohort set out. The regulations stated that if there were rail links to our destination, we could ride the trains, but only freight trains; otherwise we had to foot it along the highways. The day we took the train to Zhuzhou in Hunan province there was a torrential rainstorm.

I was sleeping in a freight car piled high with timber. I pulled a yellow tarpaulin over my blanket and enjoyed a sound night's sleep, no doubt because this was all such a novel and interesting experience.

Zhuzhou station

学生们沿公路向指定的宿营地走去

We recruits set off down the highway toward the designated camp.

At that time, the Hunan-Guangxi railroad reached only as far as the town of Yishan. After this, we marched on foot. We were two or three hundred cadets, led by an officer named Zhou. Before we set out, he divided us into small groups, allowing us to choose our groups and elect a group leader. Every day Zhou would inform the group leaders where the next night's camp would be, and every two or three days, he issued a meager allowance for food and straw sandals. He himself bought a new bicycle and raced ahead. Each group sent an advance party to arrange board and lodging for that night, while the remainder made their own way there.

I soon went through my two hundred yuan travel expenses and was forced to sell my blanket and my wristwatch.

When we got to Guiyang, I was in the advance party and stopped at a house to arrange lunch. I said I would cook, but frankly I had no idea how to go about it. Our host, a woman in her forties, took in the situation at a glance, grabbed the implements out of my hands, and started cooking.

I watched as she put rice into the pot and added water, then covered it with a small earthenware plate. Then she took a handful of sogon grass, lit it, and put it into the stove. The grass blazed, then gradually burned down, and finally went out as the rice cooked. When I thanked her, she gazed at me. "My son's enrolled at the Military Academy, just like you," she said.

进入黄埔军校的校门

Marching into the Central Military Academy, Chengdu

The banners read: "No cowards need enter here" (left). "Those looking for quick promotion and wealth, take another route" (right). "Central Military Academy" (center). Their flag reads: "Term 18 intake, First Command."

Four months later, on February 6, 1941, we finally arrived at the academy's Chengdu campus. Not one of us was missing, and when we joined new recruits from all over the country, there were around two thousand of us making up the Central Military Academy, First Command, Term 18 intake.

Six months of cadet training began. Everyone had his head shaved. I was initially put into the infantry and went to train at the Caotang Temple on the outskirts of the city.

First Command was made up of six infantry units, two cavalry units, two artillery units, two supply units, and one communications unit. Once we had completed our cadet training, we were allocated to the division we had chosen.

入伍生训练

Cadet training in front of the Caotang Temple

I admired Napoleon and chose the artillery. But they were oversubscribed, so they made us take tests in geometry and trigonometry. I was never much good at math, but I had a good memory and I simply memorized everything before the test. Sure enough, I passed and was accepted into the artillery course.

In February 1943, our cohort, First Command, Term 18, was about to graduate when I received a letter from home telling me that my mother had passed away in the autumn of 1942. I was distraught.

砲科訓練

Artillery training

When we were asked where we wanted to go after graduation, the others chose units which had first-class equipment, but I simply chose the 100th Army, stationed in Yong-feng county, in my home province of Jiangxi. Come what may, I was determined to go home first and pay my respects at my mother's grave. After that, I would go and kill the enemy, and die without regret.

I did as I had planned, returning to Nancheng first, and then going with Third Brother to Magu Mountain to pay my respects at my mother's grave. After a couple of weeks, I enlisted with the 100th Army, who by that time were in Liuyang county, Hunan province.

Paying my respects at my mother's grave

LEFT The grave of Yuan Jia (née Yang). RIGHT The grave of Rao Zhixiang.

常德外圍之戰

The Battle of Changde, Hunan province

In November of that year, during the Changde Campaign, the 100th Army received orders to come to the aid of our troops there. We arrived at the Jinlan Temple near Yiyang city, took over a memorial hall, and, after a brief rest and reorganization, went three or four li down the road to where the battle raged. The sound of machine guns grew louder and more insistent, and, as soon as we arrived on the scene, we launched an attack on the mountaintop occupied by the Japanese army. Intense firing went on until four o'clock in the afternoon, when the gunfire died away. A platoon cook bringing food, seeing that all was quiet, went up our mountain to take a look at the mountain opposite. I heard a single gunshot as he was hit in the head by a Japanese sniper. He died instantly. I remember only that his surname was Ren.

That was my first experience of combat with the Japanese.

衡阳外围喝稻田水

Drinking water in the paddy fields around Hengyang

In June 1944, at the Battle of Hengyang in Hunan, the 100th Army received orders to advance as far as Sitang, forty li beyond Hengyang. Our advance troops were being held at bay by the Japanese; the rearguard awaited orders on the highway. From eight in the morning until four or five in the afternoon, we waited. Under the scorching sun, I became unbearably thirsty. Finally, I used my enamel mug to scoop out some muddy yellow-brown water from the nearby paddy fields and followed that with two slices of raw garlic. The water tasted indescribably delicious and did me no harm at all.

湘西会战中我对日寇突然袭击

Launching a surprise attack on the Japs during the West Hunan Campaign

The West Hunan Campaign took place in the summer of 1945. The battle began on April 9 and ended on June 7. On the morning of April 19, I was on Yu Lin Dong (Fish-scale Cave) Mountain and spotted a large force of Japanese troops on the mountain opposite, moving in the direction of the Zhijiang River, some on horseback, some being carried in covered and open sedan chairs. They were about a kilometer away, well out of mortar range. So I flouted regulations and moved two field guns to the front line on the slope. We took aim and fired more than a hundred rounds of shells. Plumes of black smoke billowed into the air. The Japanese were caught completely off guard. They were unable to fire back because they could not see how many of us there were, so they just had to take cover. When we had finished firing, I had the field guns taken back to their position on the other side of the mountain and found a cottage where I could take a rest. Toward evening, a civilian came over from the opposite mountain to give me the good news: "This morning's volley was spot-on! Seventy Japanese devils killed or wounded, including the brigade commander!"

The next morning, I again saw the Japanese marching over the opposite mountain. On impulse (I was very young), I set up the field guns in the same place as yesterday, hoping for another surprise attack. But this time the enemy was prepared. We had fired only a couple of rounds when their heavy machine guns strafed our position, and we were hit by small arms fire as well. This time, it was we who were completely exposed, pinned down under enemy fire. I gave the order to dismantle the field guns and take cover. As the bullets rained down, I suddenly heard a scream; the leader of Squad 4, Li Ashui, who was lying ten paces to my right, had been hit. Within a few minutes, he was gone.

I looked up at the sky. It was a bright sunny day, with a few lingering clouds casting shadows. I gazed at the green mountains all around. Amid the bombardment, I thought to myself: Blue sky, white clouds, verdant mountains, if I end up buried here, so be it.

山头受围，九死一生

Pinned down on the mountain, a narrow escape

日军逃军时留有掩护部队

As the Japanese fled, they left soldiers to cover their retreat.

After a while, when the enemy saw no movement, they stopped firing, and we quickly retreated, but at the first signs of movement, the firing began again, and we took cover. This was repeated several times until we finally reached the mountaintop and then our encampment on the other side. That evening, our comrades took shovels and we buried Li Ashui where he had fallen. He was scarcely twenty years old, and I remember he was from Ningbo. In the words of the poet:

故軍逃竄時沿途丟 紙片

Routed enemy troops dropped scraps of paper along their way.

A hero has no need to be buried in his native place.
He lies surrounded by green mountains.[12]

For a few days, we pursued the Japanese army as far as Guanyin Mountain. The Japanese left small units in the rear to cover their retreat, and we were frequently ambushed when we reached strategic passes or wooded areas.

追击途中恶臭难闻

There was a terrible stench as we pursued the enemy through the villages.

The Japanese usually retreated under cover of darkness and used to tear up their notebooks and scatter the scraps of paper along the path so that stragglers could follow and catch up with the main force. The practice marked their route for us too, as we pursued them.

As we trailed them, there was an awful smell, because the Japanese, who had run out of rations, killed the oxen to feed the troops, leaving carcasses that quickly putrefied in the summer heat.

At perhaps nine o'clock in the morning one day, we launched an attack on Guanyin Mountain.

The Japanese had left a covering force at the peak. I set up the mortars on a mountain facing them, less than two hundred meters away. First we shelled their peak, then half an hour later, our infantry scaled the peak and I extended our firing range to cut off the enemy's retreat.

The mountain was very steep and not easy to climb. It took until five o'clock in the afternoon before Sergeant Zhao, of the 2nd Platoon, 7th Company, 3rd Battalion, was able to scale it on his own and seize the gun barrel of the Japanese machine gunner. Immediately, a rifleman to his left shot at him. The bullet glanced off the side of his head and knocked him into a Japanese foxhole. If only we had had metal helmets, he would not have died, but our equipment was very poor, and some soldiers had no more than cloth caps.

攻占观音山时的瞬间所见

Briefly glimpsed as we attacked Guanyin Mountain

Five or six minutes later, I arrived with the artillery platoon. We had routed the Japanese, and all that remained on the narrow top of the mountain were empty foxholes. In one of them lay the corpse of a hirsute Japanese soldier; he had a mustache and full beard, and his hairy chest was exposed. The mountainside was covered with shell cases. Sergeant Zhao lay to one side, an enemy soldier's corpse at his feet. I paused for a brief moment, taking in the jade-green mountains around us, the utter silence, the lingering wisps of gun smoke, the blood-red setting sun. Then we hurriedly descended and continued our pursuit.

By the beginning of June 1945, it was clear that the Japanese army was losing the West Hunan Campaign. The remaining soldiers retreated to Shaoyang city and refused to come out.

Three kilometers from the west gate of Shaoyang was a mountain called Da Shan Ling (Big Ridge). This was a strategic stronghold, and the Japanese had built extensive fortifications there. The 188th Regiment of the 63rd Division had been attacking it for two weeks without success. At the beginning of July, the 189th Regiment was ordered to send a battalion to attack it. My artillery platoon was ordered into action, and the Allies sent twenty planes from the Flying Tigers squadron to assist.

平如 2010.10.24.

At six o'clock in the morning, the mortars were in position. At eight o'clock the Flying Tigers arrived, and our troops put out white boards as markers. The fighter planes dropped firebombs, then circled, dived, and strafed the Japanese fortifications. Fire erupted from the mountaintop, but there was no movement from the Japanese. Our artillery company formed the vanguard, first firing a hundred shells, then extending our range so that a platoon of thirty or so infantrymen could go on the attack. They made no headway. Japanese soldiers were extremely well trained and had made ample preparation for close-range shooting. At midday, I was summoned to the battalion commander. He had received orders from the top brass that we had better retake the peak by the afternoon, or heads would roll. "Young man, you've got to do your bit!" he told me as he ate his pumpkin and pickled vegetables.

By four or five in the afternoon, we still had not done it. Far away, I caught sight of a dozen or so of our infantrymen sprawled in the undergrowth. One was wearing a white shirt, no doubt stolen from a Japanese soldier. They had been there all afternoon, quite motionless, long dead.

This was only a month or so before our victory in the War Against Japan.

In 2008, my son Guobin accompanied me back to those battlegrounds, and this time I climbed the peak we had not been able to conquer then. The Japanese trenches were still there. I stood in silence and laid flowers in honor of those who had given their lives that day; they were the unknown soldiers—their families probably never knew that they had been killed there.

After this campaign, we remained stationed on the outskirts of Shaoyang city. On August 13, we heard the news that an atomic bomb had been dropped on Japan. Shortly afterward, the Japanese surrendered unconditionally, and the 188th Regiment sent envoys into the city to receive their surrender. The troops were jubilant, and the local inhabitants organized a great parade to celebrate.

We had won.

Before I met Meitang, I had no fear of dying, or of long journeys, and was blithely unconcerned with the passage of the years. But now, I began to consider the future very carefully indeed.

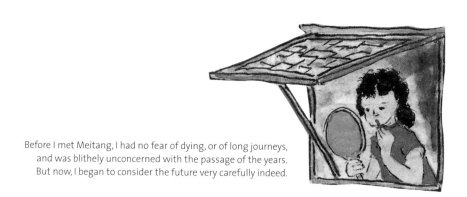

3
A Dab of Red Lipstick

When the war ended, in the spring of 1946, I was twenty-five years old and a first lieutenant spotter in the artillery battalion, 63rd Brigade, of the 83rd Division. Our troops were then stationed in Taizhou city, before being moved to the town of Taixing, also in Jiangsu province, in the summer. About that time, I received a letter from my father, the gist of which was that my younger brother, Shouru, was getting married. He hoped I could get home for the occasion, and he wanted to take the opportunity, while I was home, to arrange a marriage for me too.

We had been talking about my marriage for some years. The first time was when I graduated from the Military Academy and happened to be passing through Ganzhou city, where my father had rented a house in Canfu Qian Street for his law practice. A neighbor, a businessman also from Nancheng county, had a daughter. My father and my aunt made arrangements for me to have lunch with the father and the daughter. All I remember is that the daughter had a very round, chubby face.

That was the summer when I went home to pay my respects at my mother's grave. Afterward, I accompanied my father back to Nancheng. My father had an old friend, a man named Xie Houzu, who was a practitioner of Chinese medicine. He had several daughters, one of whom, an upper middle school student, they wished to introduce to me. However, I felt that as I was about to enter the army and go to the front line, it was not the right time to be talking about marriage, so I turned them down too.

But now we had won the War Against Japan, and when my father raised the subject of marriage again, I was happy to go along with it.

It was not easy to get a leave of absence in those days; the brigade commander had to approve your application, and the chances of getting that approval were slim. But then my battalion commander, Liu Hengxin, found out what was afoot. He was a forthright and decisive man, and took it upon himself to give me two weeks' leave without reporting it to the commander.

离开泰兴, 踏上回家旅途之早晨所见

In the early morning, I left Taixing to return home.

I got along very well with several of the young men in my battalion: Sun Yi (the quartermaster), Ye Yinmin (aide-de-camp), Peng Shanhe (in charge of ordnance), and Zhu Baoqing (in charge of bedding and clothing). Peng and Zhu later went to Taiwan, along with Liu, who departed in 1948. Later, Peng sent me a photograph of us in military uniform. (All my old army photographs have long since been burned.) We all enjoyed one another's company and often went for a stroll through the streets of Taizhou, visited the public baths, or had a meal together in a restaurant. On the eve of my departure for home, these friends gave me a farewell dinner. I got so drunk I fell asleep at the table. Early the next morning, I threw a few things together and set out, with enough money for my travel expenses and a Japanese sword—a war memento presented to me by the battalion commander. I was in such a hurry to be off that I actually put on the wrong boots. The battalion commander had presented both Sun Yi and me with pairs of short, dark tan leather boots, made to order by a cobbler. They were identical, except that Sun's were a fraction smaller. It was only when I had left the camp that I realized the right boot was a bit tight. But there was nothing to be done, I just had to put up with the discomfort.

The sun had risen by the time I reached the town's south gate. There was no one around, just two sentries on guard. Many years of war had deprived the town of its trees, and it looked bleak, with only earthen walls and fortified towers, dusty roads and the shapes of houses in the distance. In the words of the Song dynasty lament by Jiang Kui: "Abandoned ponds and lofty trees still detest talk of soldiers."[13]

I planned to take a boat from Zhenjiang to Jiujiang in Jiangxi province. It was eight or nine at night by the time I arrived in Zhenjiang. The harsh lights of the dock area shone up into the sky as I walked down the paved road to the jetty and boarded the paddle steamer bound for Jiujiang. It was a hot August night, and few of the passengers wanted to go below. Instead, they sat or lay on deck with their bags spread around them, enjoying the cool breeze.

They were too noisy for me, so I went below to find a bunk. I have a vague recollection of a round porthole, through which I could hear hawkers on deck selling food, but I was exhausted, and soon fell asleep.

After the boat docked at Jiujiang, I took a train to Nanchang city, and then went straight to Number 18, Chenjia Bridge. The next morning, my father and I took a long-distance bus to Linchuan—I had only two weeks' leave and my father was in a hurry. It was late at night by the time we arrived, and we checked into the Gaosheng Inn.

Once we were settled, my father told me a bit about the family of the girl in question; Mr. Mao Sixiang was a close friend, and they were well off. The next day, we went to Meitang's house.

晚间走下镇江码头，登上开赴九江的大轮船佗。

In the evening, I went down to the dock at Zhenjiang and boarded a large paddle steamer to Jiujiang.

The Gaosheng Inn

It was large. We walked through two courtyards and were about to enter the main hall of the third when I suddenly saw a small window in the west building open. I looked more closely—there was a pretty young woman about twenty years old holding a hand mirror to the light in her right hand and applying lipstick with her left. She did not see me, but I knew it must be her. That was my first real impression of Meitang.

08.6.10. 平如 [seal]

第一次看到美棠时之印象

My first glimpse of Meitang

It was a lovely day, with a warm southerly breeze that caressed our faces. I did not stop, just followed my father into the hall. Mr. Mao and his wife welcomed us, and called Meitang to come and meet me.

After a short while, my father brought out a gold ring, which my mother must have bought with my engagement in mind. He gave it to Mr. Mao, and he, in turn, took it to Meitang, who was sitting on the bamboo couch, and slipped it onto her finger. And so we were engaged.

My father gave the engagement ring to Mr. Mao.

We chatted over our meal. My future father-in-law urged us to have more chicken soup, and then turned to me and asked, "Would you like a cigarette? A drink?" I said I did not smoke or drink. In fact, that was not entirely true, but this was a special occasion and I felt no need to answer in too much detail. "Excellent! Excellent!" he responded.

He and my father began to reminisce about old times, and I took the opportunity to look around me. Meitang and Youtang (then twelve years old) sat on the bamboo couch, while the remaining three siblings—Shuntang, Xiaotang, and Aitang—sat together on low stools, regarding me with great curiosity.

The evening was drawing in, and my father took his leave and set off for the Gao-sheng Inn. The following day he was returning to Nanchang city. But I stayed on so that I could have some time with Meitang and play with the children. Meitang showed me a big package full of photographs she had had taken in Hankou, and I picked a few to take with me. One of them, the one Meitang herself liked the most, was a twelve-inch color portrait. I planned to take it back to my regiment and have some smaller prints made to present to my army friends.

I commented on how thin Meitang was, and she told me she had had a bout of malaria and had only just recovered. Although she was still convalescing, she was in high spirits. She loved to sing, and she rolled up old newspapers to act as a megaphone and sang us popular songs: "Life Is Wonderful," "The Phoenix Takes Wing," "Fragrant Nights," "Don't Forget Tonight," "Flying All Over the Dance Floor," "Express Train," and many more.

I stayed the night, and two of the women, "Sister Peng" and "Sister Lianfa," made up a bed for me. Lianfa was actually a concubine of Meitang's older cousin, Yu Xiu'an, but had quarreled with his wife, Dong Yun, and was staying in Meitang's house in the meantime. The two women put a bamboo couch for me in a large east-side room, gave me a mat and a pillow, and placed a lighted mosquito coil by the bed. Later, Meitang repeated to me what Lianfa had said that evening: "I specially sprinkled plenty of toilet water on his pillow!" Apart from my bed, the room was completely empty. I lay down, but my head was too full of thoughts for me to sleep. Meitang's family had rented this house in Linchuan because her mother's brother, Li Yuansheng, was a famous physician. My future in-laws were in their fifties and wanted to live close to him, in case they needed medical care. Meitang had no elder brother, just a string of younger siblings in the process of growing up. I was about to become "Big Brother-in-Law," on hand to help care for this family and guide the young ones toward adulthood. This was no small responsibility.

As soon as it got light, I went out to explore my surroundings. The main west-side rooms were occupied by my future parents-in-law, while the other members of the family had a number of rooms at the back. In one courtyard, steps led up to the reception room. Rooms flanked it on both sides: the east-side ones were full of old junk, while Yutang, Meitang's elder sister, lived on the west side. Yutang was now twenty-four years old. She was still chronically ill and depressed, and kept to her room. Unaware of this, I pushed open her door. She lay on the messy bed, face to the wall, a painfully skinny figure covered with a thin coverlet embroidered with cheerful red flowers. She looked so pitiable that I quickly withdrew.

At the back of the courtyard was a dividing wall with a door on the east side and, beyond that, a small garden. Covered walkways ran along the east and south walls, while the west and north walls were simply whitewashed. The garden was planted with flowers and shrubs, and there was a large ceramic fishbowl and stone benches. The effect was quite charming. A sturdy pomelo tree grew in the center of the garden, and I was told I could eat its fruit. However, everything had an air of neglect: there were weeds, bits of rubble, and broken paving stones, among which the dozen or so hens my future mother-in-law kept scratched around happily.

2008.6.17

临川美棠家住宅之示意图

Sketch of Meitang's family residence in Linchuan

1. Entrance. 2. Dining table and chairs. 3. Bamboo couch. 4. Stools. 5. My in-laws' rooms. 6. Family rooms. 7. Empty rooms. 8. Small courtyard. 9. Yutang's room. 10. Storeroom. 11. Covered walkways. 12. Pomelo tree. 13. Flock of hens. 14. Large goldfish bowl.

On the third day, the whole family got ready to set off for Nanchang city for the wedding of my younger brother, Shouru. In Nanchang, my parents-in-law stayed at the Jiangxi Hotel, but Meitang stayed with my sister Ding's husband's family because their house was nearer our home, and she came over every morning to help with the preparations. On the day of the wedding, all the women guests crowded into the room to watch the bride get ready. Meitang, in particular, had always loved beauty products and fashionable clothes, and she made herself very popular by helping the bride with her makeup and her hair, and giving her advice on choosing the bridal jewelry.

1946年夏天，南昌繁华路段的街景

Busy streets in Nanchang city, in the summer of 1946

Text on signs: "Everything at twenty percent discount" (left); "Prices slashed for 100 days" (right)

南昌著名的点心 —— 吊炉烧饼

A well-known Nanchang snack food, "ovenside sesame cakes"

美棠和我常到湖滨公园去乘凉

Meitang and I often strolled in Lakeside Park to enjoy the cool air.

白石为凭，明月为证，我心早相许，
今後天涯，愿长相忆，爱心永不移。

平如

1946年夏天的南昌湖滨公园

Lakeside Park, Nanchang city in the summer of 1946

"White rocks and the moon are our witnesses, our hearts are promised to each other
No matter when and where we are, we will never forget, our love will be steadfast."[14]

在四照楼露天茶座品茶

In the Sizhao open-air tea garden

After dinner every evening, Meitang and I went out and strolled along Nanchang's two busiest streets, Ximachi (Horse-washing Pond) and Zhongshan Road, stopping every now and then to buy some small items or eat snacks.

At the east end of Ximachi, there were no shops and the crowds thinned out. Then if you walked a bit farther, there was Lakeside Park. The lake in question was Nanchang's East Lake, which was very large and had a pavilion in the middle. Mature trees lined the lakeside, their interlaced branches blotting out the sky. Every evening we strolled there, enjoying the almost magical effect created by the streetlamps shining through the gathering dusk. The park also had an open-air tea garden, a particularly secluded spot. The seating area was decorated with strings of colored lightbulbs hung between the trees, and furnished with cane chairs and tea tables. There Meitang and I sat chatting and sipping our tea until late at night.

On one occasion, Ding and her husband, and his elder brother, Luo Jingqing, invited us to the Sizhao, then Nanchang's best-known teahouse. It was on two floors, with an outdoor area open in summer, decorated with lights and furnished with rattan chairs like the teahouse in Lakeside Park, but offering a greater variety of teas and sweet snacks. We chatted, drank, and nibbled as a fresh breeze wafted over us, almost unaware of the passing of time. When it came time to leave, I was quite determined that I would pay the bill (about two silver dollars), even though we were there at the invitation of Luo Jingqing. Meitang always teased me about that incident—she said it showed how very unsophisticated I was back then.

2008.7.

我站在九江开往镇江的轮船甲板上，看着
那"滚滚长江东逝水"，憧憬着未来

Standing on the deck of the paddle steamer heading back to
Zhenjiang, I watched the Yangtze River waters rolling eastward,
my head full of dreams of the future.

把美棠的照片拿给战友们看

Showing Meitang's picture to my comrades

My brother's wedding was over, and my leave was also coming to an end. Meitang returned with her family to Linchuan, and I took her photograph back with me to my barracks. The artillery battalion of the 63rd Brigade had moved back to Taizhou, so I retraced my steps:

I went first by paddle steamer from Jiujiang to Zhenjiang, embarking this time at ten in the morning. I stood on the deck watching the passing scenery, listening to the long-drawn-out blasts of the ship's horn. Boats passed back and forth across the river, their sails reflected on the waters, which glittered in the bright sunlight. The river and the steamer were the same as before, but the thoughts that filled my heart could not have been more different. Before I met Meitang, I had no fear of dying, or of long journeys, and was blithely unconcerned about the passage of the years. But now, I began to consider the future very carefully indeed.

Back at the barracks, the first thing I did was to take out my pictures of my fiancée and show them around to my comrades.

The artillery battalion was now stationed in Jichuan township outside the South Gate of Taizhou city. Our barracks were really very nice. In every courtyard, bonsai trees were displayed on stands. The timber beams and doorposts of the buildings were painted dark red, and the beams were decorated with carvings. We had the impression that our landlord was very well off. My room was a small reception room on the left as you entered. I stuck the twelve-inch color photograph of Meitang on the east wall. My bed was against the wall, and I had a redwood table beside it, on which I wrote my letters to her. I filled three or four pages in every letter, telling her what was going on, and my plans for the future, before consigning it to the army mail. The landlord's daughter was sixteen years old and in junior middle school. She was rather short, plump, and fair-skinned, and she often dropped by my room to chat artlessly about this and that. I never invited her to sit down, so she would stand on the other side of the table to talk to me. Then one day she noticed the photograph on the wall and asked me who it was. "My fiancée," I said. She never came back after that.

The atmosphere in the platoon at that time was gloomy. The elation that had followed our victory over Japan quickly dissipated, and rumors settled oppressively over us. We heard that negotiations between the Kuomintang and the Communists had broken down and that another war was imminent. And indeed civil war soon broke out. The entire 83rd Division was ordered north, and one afternoon in early autumn every company in the artillery battalion of the 63rd Brigade set out.

The townsfolk, with whom we got along very well, came to bid us sad farewells. I was the last to leave. Mounting my much-loved Australian warhorse, branded with the number 35, I took a last look at Taizhou's South Gate outlined in the gloom. I felt that I would probably never come back here again.

2009.9.30.平如

損，而可謂奇遇矣。

的棉大衣胸前毋貫穿二孔，劉竟毫髮無

起身之時忽有一流彈自窗口射來，將劉

觀察前方戰況，就在我们二人均坐下當未

竹棚中相對而坐，輪流从觀測器材中

在盐城之役，營長劉恆鑫與我一

作抵抗。

直退到山東臨沂，仅使用小部队暑

密轉移，其主力向高郵、淮阴、盐城一

公路向蘇北推進，莹則采取戰

2008.10.9. 平如

As the 83rd Division pushed into the north of Jiangsu province, the People's Liberation Army (PLA) adopted diversionary tactics: their main force withdrew to the towns of Gaoyou, Huaiyin, and Yancheng, as far as Linyi in Shandong province, while only small units remained behind to offer resistance.

One day during the Yancheng Campaign, I was with my battalion commander, Liu Hengxin, in a bamboo hut. We were keeping the battle under observation, taking turns with the field glasses. We were seated opposite each other when suddenly a bullet sped in through the window and passed between us. It left two holes in the front of Liu's padded greatcoat—but miraculously left Liu himself unscathed!

On an army march, deaths were a common occurrence, you just accepted it as the will of heaven, and made no fuss about it. Once, when our company was in Yancheng, Liu Hengxin and I were in a field of sorghum and had chosen a bamboo hut to serve as an observation post. The hut had a window, about forty centimeters square, and I erected the observation equipment there. I sat opposite Liu, and we took turns going to the window to make our observations. The terrain was fairly level, with only low dikes and hillocks, so we were completely exposed. Suddenly we were sprayed with bullets that landed all around the hut. I had been about to get up to go to the window, and Liu had just moved away from the window, when a bullet entered and passed between us, piercing his coat on the right and exiting on the left. It made two neat holes in the fabric, but somehow missed Liu completely.

In the winter of 1946, the 83rd Division arrived in Linyi in Shandong, to find the city completely empty. I explored every street and alley and failed to find a single person. But the walls were covered in slogans, declaring that the Kuomintang forces did not want to fight and that the Communist PLA treated all their captives leniently, whether an army, a brigade, or an individual. About two weeks after we arrived, the local inhabitants began to trickle back and city life returned to normal. The 63rd Brigade received orders to defend the city and strengthen its defenses.

Before long, it was the Spring Festival. We were all extremely anxious; we had been on the battlefield for years and, while we had never shirked our duty to defend our people against the Japanese invaders, the enemy were now gone, and all we wanted to do was return home and be with our loved ones. We had never expected a new war to flare up. We had no idea how long it would last, or where it would take us, and, at least among us ordinary soldiers, there was an intense reluctance to go on fighting. Early in the morning of New Year's Day, I was in the courtyard when I heard sporadic gunfire all around the city, bangs mixed with the rattle of light machine-gun fire. It was the soldiers firing into the sky because they had no firecrackers to welcome in the New Year. Of course, this was against army regulations, but their immediate superiors were taking a relaxed attitude. Human nature and human feelings are very much the same everywhere. After the New Year, there were major changes in the battalion, and one afternoon in early spring, I found myself walking into a mud-brick compound on East Street, Linyi, and being introduced to the entire company by the commander of the 3rd Battalion, 189th Regiment, Pu Yunlong: "I've found you the best possible company commander," he said.

When you invited guests for a meal, the food was simple, stir-fried shredded pork and greens, eggs fried with garlic chives, and the like. You would order half a jin of baijiu liquor too, and everyone would down several measures.

More and more soldiers were deserting; the rank and file were not treated well, arms and equipment were poor, as were living conditions, and sometimes we even went short of food. But troop numbers were reported just as before, a practice called "eating vacancies," and the resulting extra provisions, food, bedding, and uniforms were siphoned off by those in charge. They could get away with it provided they kept within limits. Such graft was tacitly accepted as a perk—because it did not involve depriving the foot soldiers of their rations. Of course, how much misreporting went on depended on military rank; a senior officer could get away with fabricating an entire guard regiment.

临沂北门一家饭店——我常之请客的地方

TEXT AT RIGHT A restaurant at North Gate, Linyi city. I often invited friends here.

When I was still artillery platoon leader, I would claim for an extra five or six in addition to the sixty or so officers and men under me. I simply added all the extra provisions to the men's rations and asked them if that was enough. If it was not enough, then I claimed for a few more, telling them it was me who would be in the firing line if it came to that. When they said they had full bellies, I stopped doing it. In actual fact, of course, I never had to face the firing squad.

As a result, I never had a single deserter from my platoon from 1944 on, and I earned a reputation as a worker of small miracles.

Pu Yunlong had heard of my reputation too, hence his flattering introduction. It had never occurred to me, however, that I was any kind of "best possible company commander." If you wanted men to give their lives fighting for their country, you had to give them enough to eat. That was all there was to it.

At the beginning of summer in 1947, under General Tang Enbo, the 74th Division occupied the Mount Mengliang uplands, while the 83rd and 25th Divisions occupied the peaks to left and right in the rear to offer protection. The 63rd Brigade received orders to go up into the mountains. For about a month, there was no movement. In those days, when our troops were not fighting and had nothing else to do, they danced, just like the American army did. Our venue was one of the reception rooms; there the floor was pretty level, and we sprinkled it with French chalk. A gramophone sat on the table by one wall, and along the wall facing the door was a bench where one could rest. We whirled merrily around the dance floor, but we also knew quite well that the top brass on both sides were playing an endgame. In the current crisis, battles could break out at any moment, and the next day might be our last.

Around then, the 63rd Brigade acquired four American 37mm antitank guns. On May 15, news came down from the brigade headquarters that I was to be appointed its antitank company commander, with horses and men to be transferred from other companies. I was to return to Linyi city forthwith, to pick up ammunition and equipment from the depot, and then to go and train my troops. On May 16, at the crack of dawn, I set off with my men. We wasted no time and by midday were passing through a large village called Guanzhuang. We were still only halfway to Linyi when we saw trucks of the 83rd Division, coming in the opposite direction, from Linyi, transporting supplies to the front line.

At two o'clock in the afternoon, things took an unexpected turn. We saw the trucks driving back to Linyi—they had turned around. They told us that Guanzhuang village had been occupied by the PLA, and they could not get through. This meant that supply lines to the 83rd were cut, and they were surrounded. As it transpired, on the fifteenth, the same evening that I handed over to Company Commander Lou, the PLA launched an attack on the 83rd in order to prevent them from coming to the aid of the 74th. By then, the 74th had been surrounded on Mount Mengliang for four days, and had exhausted their ammunition, food, and water, and the 83rd was now too busy saving themselves to come to their comrades' aid.

It was early summer and very hot. My company hurried to Linyi, arriving at five in the afternoon.

It had been a fine and sunny day, but just as we arrived the weather suddenly changed: dense black clouds gathered overhead and a gale blew up. Sand swirled in the air and rumbles of thunder drew nearer. Then there was a sudden burst of hailstones that drummed deafeningly on the roofs.

Roofs in the north are lower than southern roofs; I stood under the eaves watching hailstones bigger than soybeans falling on the tiles of the hall opposite, then bouncing seventy or eighty centimeters up into the air. A little while later, a soldier from the 74th Division antitank company turned up. He had escaped the encirclement and told us that the 74th had been completely annihilated: ten senior officers—including its commander, Zhang Lingfu, his deputy, his chief of staff, and his chief of staff's deputy—had all written suicide notes and given them to a staff officer who managed to break through enemy lines and reach the rear. Apparently when the PLA were no more than two hundred meters away, the commanding officers, including Zhang Lingfu, had lined up and Zhang had ordered one of their number to shoot everybody, one by one. The officer executing the order had then shot himself. The brigade, regiment, and battalion commanders, and even the platoon commanders and their soldiers, had followed suit, either killing themselves or fighting to the death. It must have been an appalling scene.

The hailstorm lasted two hours before abating. Later my orderly, Chen Xusheng, used to joke: "Commander Rao's a lucky man! He spends a month or so at the foot of the mountain and nothing happens! And the very evening he hands over to Commander Lou, disaster strikes!" If I had had only myself to think about, I would have considered myself fortunate to be killed in battle. It is glorious to die on the battlefield, as the ancients used to say. But then Meitang's and my story would have stopped right there. And fate decreed otherwise . . . maybe we really were meant to marry.

When hostilities abated, Meitang and I continued to write to each other, and sometimes she sent photographs. I had begun to feel that I was not at all happy to be fighting my fellow country people—I had joined up to fight the Japanese, after all. The regulations forbade any officer with soldiers under him to take leave, but it was easy enough to get leave if one was a staff officer.

I was then mortar company commander of the 56th Regiment, 19th Brigade. I was on good terms with the chief of staff, Shi Zhiguang. I told him that I wanted to transfer

中汤于精味加光之史

Shi Zhiguang adding MSG to the soup

to brigade headquarters as a staff officer. Of course, after a month, I planned to request leave to get married. Shi Zhiguang agreed immediately and reported this to Brigade Commander Zhao Yao.

Zhao was happy to have me on board and immediately gave the order for my transfer. I set off to report at the brigade headquarters, accompanied only by my orderly, Chen Xusheng. Just before my departure, the entire mortar company lined up to see me off. My commander choked up, I saw some of the soldiers' eyes fill with tears, and I was almost overcome with emotion as well.

The staff officers' camp had no ways of boosting its income and rations, so food was in very short supply. For a month, I ate no meat or fish. Apart from vegetables, there was only egg soup. Our chief of staff, Shi Zhiguang, tried his best to do something about it. Before every meal, he would hurry to his room and fetch a small bottle of MSG and sprinkle a small spoonful in the soup. He had no money to buy us more food, and could only add a little extra flavor.

When the month was nearly up, I put in a written request to go home to get married, and Shi Zhiguang signed off on it and passed it up to Zhao Yao. Zhao immediately approved it, and, two days later, the brigade headquarters personnel office issued me a leave certificate. This was a formal travel pass, complete with the brigade's official seal and Zhao's signature and personal seal.

The very next day, the 19th Brigade received an order to go immediately to Xuzhou Airport, to be flown to Jinan to come to the aid of Wang Yaowu's army. They were besieged in Jinan, and the 19th was Wang's old headquarters. The 19th could not get through overland, so air was the only option.

Zhao Yao said to me: "There's no need for you to go! Go home." If that order had come three days earlier, I most certainly would not have been bold enough to apply for home leave. And in that case, too, the story of us two would have been very different, or indeed there might have been no story to write at all.

That same evening, all the men of the brigade boarded the train for Xuzhou. Chen and I, carrying our small bundles, got on a goods carriage at the very end of the train. It was completely empty.

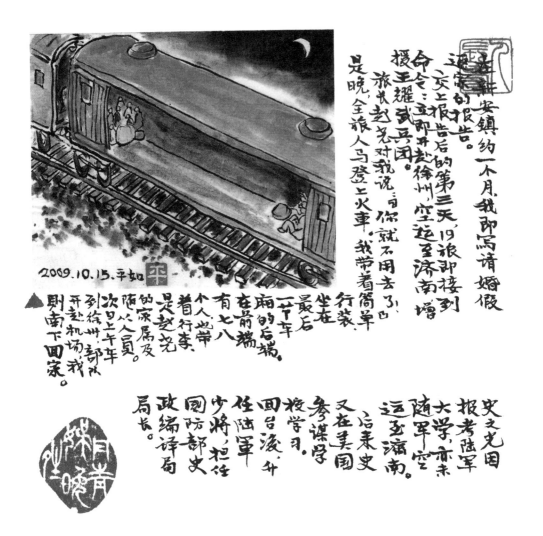

迁家约一个月，我即写请婚假迁交上报告后的第三天，19旅即接到命令：立即开赴徐州空运至济南增援王耀武兵团。旅长赵志光对我说："你，就不用去了。"是晚，全旅人马登上火车。我带着简单行装，坐在最后一节车厢的后端。在前端，有七、八个人，也带着行李。是赵志光的家属及随从人员。次旦上午，到徐州，部队则南下回家。

史之光因报考陆军大学，亦未随军空运至济南。后来史又在美国参谋学校学习，回台湾后，升少将，担任国防部史政编译局局长。

2009.10.15. 平如 平

The next day around ten in the morning, the train pulled into Xuzhou station. The 19th Brigade went straight to the airport, and Zhao Yao's family hurried off to their destination. Chen and I took a train to Nanjing and then boarded a train to Nanchang city, in my home province of Jiangxi. I arrived there in July 1948.

It was arranged that Meitang and I would wed in the middle of the eighth lunar month, and we needed to start making preparations. Our new home would be the west-side rooms in the third courtyard. The paint was flaking, and I set to and gave it two coats of whitewash. I pasted newspaper over the back wall so it looked a little better. My father and aunt bought us two new pieces of furniture: a new-style wooden bed and a five-drawer chest. They also gave us some pieces of their own: a side table, a round dining table, and some chairs. We did not anticipate that we would be living there for long.

Author's note: I learned later what befell the 19th on their journey. Zhou Zhengzhong, of the 56th Regiment, which was holding the South Gate, was cut down by submachine gunfire. A fellow student of mine, Guo Xianzong, was commander of the 7th Battalion, and we had stayed in touch because we were from the same town and school. He was hit by a shell and blown to smithereens. A man who was our quartermaster in Zhouzhen town, whom I had played basketball with, was taken prisoner. Zhao Yao managed to get away and fled to Taiwan, where his wife made flatbreads and fried bread-sticks, and they eked out a living running a small eatery until, a few years later, Taiwan's economy fortunately picked up. Shi Zhiguang had been accepted at the Army College and did not go to Jinan. Instead he went to America and graduated from a staff college before going to Taiwan.

美棠和我在洗马池买瓷器

Meitang and I bought ceramics in Ximachi. Signs read: "Genuine goods at fair prices" (left); "Famous Jingdezhen ceramics" (right).

One day, a platoon commander from the mortar company of the 63rd Brigade, a man called Su Liansheng, dropped by the house with some news. Fifty or sixty officers from the 63rd were just then passing through Nanchang city. They were billeted in the Xin Yuan Middle School and would stay for a month or so. The next day I went over to talk to them and reminisce about the old days, and, when they heard about my wedding, they presented me with a plaque.

A few days later, my sister Ding and I went to Linchuan to escort Meitang and her family to Nanchang. Her dowry was almost ready, but there were a few small things still to get, so once again, we found ourselves strolling down Ximachi to make the remaining purchases.

美棠和我买回来的"古董"饭碗

The "antique" bowls Meitang and I bought

One day we were there with my younger brother and his wife and baby Yinzeng, then just a year old. We were about to go into a china shop when Yinzeng suddenly burst into tears and refused to go through the door. So the three of them had to wait outside. Meitang and I went in and chose two rather expensive rice bowls and spoons. To our surprise, when we got home with our purchases, my father-in-law had a good laugh at us. Apparently, in our ignorance of ceramics, we had bought outmoded "antique-style" bowls. We took his teasing in good fun.

On another occasion, my in-laws were at the Xinya Restaurant eating snacks. There was food left over, but back then it was not usual to take away a "doggie bag." So my mother-in-law sent someone to our house at Chenjia Bridge to fetch me to come and eat the leftovers. I arrived to find large quantities of baozi and jiaozi dumplings, and other snacks, which I demolished, and then I insisted on paying the bill. I overheard my father-in-law say to my mother-in-law with a chuckle: "You see? You got him here and he insists on paying the bill!"

新雅飯店的早餐

Breakfast at the Xinya Restaurant

On Zhongshan Road, there was a large department store called the Guang Yi Chang, run by the Cantonese businessman Cao Langchu. He was another friend of my father's and had taken him on as the store's legal adviser. The Guang Yi Chang was divided into separate departments: brocades and silks, clothing, shoes, camera equipment, delicatessen, and so on. The delicatessen was famous throughout Nanchang for its Cantonese delicacies.

老东家

His old employer

Meitang and I went there one day with my parents-in-law to sample the Nancheng rice noodles. To our astonishment, the chef turned out to have been the head cook at my father-in-law's pharmacy in Fujian. The cook greeted us, delighted to see his old employer again, and went to the kitchen to prepare the noodles. In due course, he brought out enormous bowls, brimming with noodles and broth, on top of which lay meatballs the size of pigeons' eggs—what a way to show affection for an old friend! I still have pleasurable memories of those exceptional noodles.

Soon we would be married.

On the eve of our wedding day, I sat at the round table in our new apartment and thought of my mother. If only she were here to see me get married. She would have been so very happy, and how happy that would have made me! Overwhelmed with grief, I laid my head on the table and wept bitterly. After a while, Eighth Aunt, my mother's sister-in-law, came in. She sat opposite me for a long time, gently comforting me until I was myself again.

The next morning, everyone at the Chenjia Bridge house hurried to the Jiangxi Grand Hotel with the decorations and everything else needed for the wedding. My parents-in-law were already staying there. Meitang, escorted by my sister Ding, would get ready in a room set aside for the bride. There was a small courtyard by the hotel entrance, with a row of boutiques running down the left-hand side: a barber shop, a photography studio, and a shop hiring out wedding outfits. I went to the barber's for a last-minute haircut, while Meitang chose her wedding dress.

WEDDING INVITATION

RAO Pingru, born at the "you" hour, twenty-seventh day of the eleventh month,
eleventh year of the Republic, Nancheng county, Jiangxi province

MAO Meitang, born at the "zi" hour, fourteenth day of the fourth month,
fourteenth year of the Republic, Nancheng county, Jiangxi province

The two gentlemen, Rao Xiaomu and Mao Yisun, who introduced the couple,
are pleased to present them at their wedding,
at the fourth hour in the afternoon of the fifteenth day of the eighth month
in the thirty-seventh year of the Republic, in the Jiangxi Grand Hotel, Nanchang.

Your presence is cordially invited.

Mr. Hu Jiafeng will act as Chief Witness and hopes that both families enjoy a happy outcome
from this union; may that happiness continue for a hundred years.

The betrothed: Rao Pingru, Mao Meitang

The Chief Witness: Mr. Hu Jiafeng

The couple were introduced by: Rao Xiaomu and Mao Yisun

Presiding: Rao Xiaoqian and Mao Sixiang

The ceremony will take place on the fifteenth day
of the eighth month in the thirty-seventh year of the Republic.[15]

2008.
6.22平如

在江西大旅
社大礼堂的
婚礼上，台上
当中的是谁
婚人，时任江
西省政府主
席胡家凤；右
立者为主婚人、
或父亲；左立
者是副秘
书长谢培
峰表弟，而是
男傧相如水
女傧相如友
听表妹（今岁

二〇〇九年十月十六日
钻石婚纪念日
平如记

144 OUR STORY

The Jiangxi Grand Hotel was a Western-style building, with a spacious entrance hall two stories high. In the center was a tiered arrangement of houseplants and flowers, colonnaded walkways ran down either side, and there was a glass roof overhead. The sun shone brightly that day, illuminating the wedding scene below. The hall was decorated specially for the occasion: there was a bright red carpet underfoot, and a long rectangular table in front, covered with a red silk tablecloth. On this lay the marriage certificate, Meitang's and my seals, and ink, and at either end stood two tall red candles.

The chairman of the Jiangxi Provincial Committee, Hu Jiafeng, was to be chief witness. He was a friend of my father's—they had been classmates at Peking University of Law and Political Science. It was he who, after he was appointed chairman, had persuaded my father to do some work for him, as a result of which my father became a senator in Jiangxi province. Hu Jiafeng was known and widely respected for his financial probity. The consequence of this virtue, in his previous post as secretary-general of the provincial government, was that his family had been too poor to pay their bills and had their electricity cut off. Less than a month later, he was unexpectedly promoted to be chairman of the provincial government—and the Electricity Board hurriedly reconnected the power supply and sent a personal apology, to the huge amusement of Nanchang's citizens.

In commemoration of our diamond wedding

TEXT IN ILLUSTRATION Our wedding in the hall of the Jiangxi Grand Hotel: on the dais is the chairman of the Jiangxi Provincial Committee, Hu Jiafeng (center); my father is on the right; and the master of ceremonies on the left. Our attendants were my sixteen-year-old boy cousin Dazheng and my girl cousin Daxin, aged fourteen.

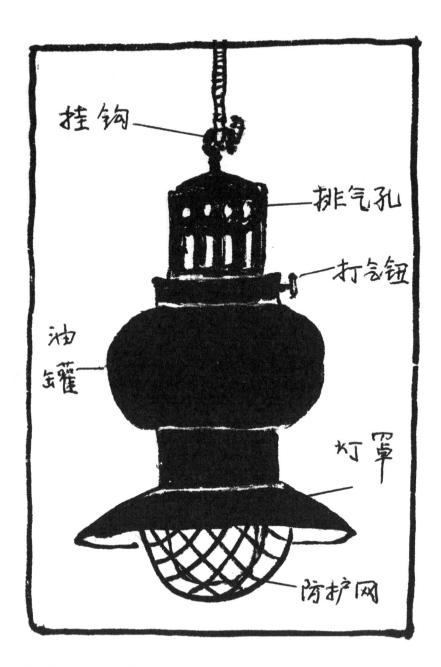

挂钩

排气孔

打气钮

油罐

灯罩

防护网

The oil lamps at the wedding

Clockwise from top: vent, pump button, shade, guard, oil tank, hook

The guests streamed in, until finally there were two hundred of them. It was the custom for the bridegroom to go in person to fetch the chief witness, and now Hu's private car was waiting. I stepped into it and we sped to the provincial government headquarters. The building was gloomy and felt like it had seen better days—it had probably started out as an imperial *yamen*.[16] Before long Hu Jiafeng emerged, dressed in a khaki Sun Yat-sen suit, and got into the car. We drove slowly to the hotel, our way impeded by crowds who wanted a glimpse of the provincial chairman. We arrived, and my father and his friends were there to greet us. The arrival of the witness created a little eddy of pleasurable excitement among the onlookers.

Meitang and I stood side by side below the dais. She wore a pure white wedding dress, and I was in an American-style khaki service uniform, of the type then fashionable in the military. Behind us stood our attendants, my boy cousin Dazheng and girl cousin Daxin, and the photographer. Facing us, the chief witness, Hu, stood in the center with my father, who was presiding on the right, and the master of ceremonies on the left.

I still remember the words of the MC: "Chief Witness, please make your speech!" Hu Jiafeng took a sheet of paper from his pocket. Unfortunately, his congratulations were replete with classical four-character phrases, and five minutes went by without either Meitang or me understanding a word. Then it was my father's turn. He was a lawyer and had no need of notes; in fact he spoke off the cuff for nearly a quarter of an hour. Then it was "Bride and Groom, please make your bows to the chief witness," and "Bride and Groom, please put your seals on the marriage certificate!" And so we were married.

We posed for wedding photographs at the hotel entrance. The fan-shaped entrance consisted of four steps leading up to a rather narrow door, flanked by two Ionic columns. The eaves of the porch, also fan-shaped, were carved and decorated. Our wedding photograph has not survived the upheavals of the intervening sixty years, but I can still remember it being taken, and the light falling on the eaves and the pillars, as vividly as if it were yesterday.

人生有幾？余良辰
美景一夢初過。
窮通前定，何用
苦張羅。

録元好問瑯兩打新
荷曲中警句

舉行婚礼后，
美棠与我在
礼堂門口合影。
原照片早已損
毀，但脑海中
的記憶尚存。

2008.5.22. 平如

"Life does not last long and the good times pass as in a dream. Whether one is rich and honored, or poor and base, all is preordained, why waste one's energies on trying to change one's fate?"
— From the song "Heavy Rain Strikes the New Lotus Flower," by Yuan Haowen

After the marriage ceremony, Meitang and I posed for our wedding photograph. The photograph was destroyed a long time ago, but I can still visualize it clearly.

After the wedding banquet, we went back to the Chenjia Bridge house, where, as night fell, the guests crowded into our new room. It was time for the "teasing" of bride and groom. Meitang and I sat on the edge of the bed and were teased. Some of the guests wanted to know the ins and outs of our courtship, others tried to make jokes at our expense, but we dealt with them easily.

The trickiest was my elder sister's husband, Luo Jingqing—in the picture, he is the lanky fellow in the checked gown. My own big brother—the bald man in the blue gown—joined in just as enthusiastically, but he was there not to tease us but to extricate us from our predicament.

闹新房的场面

Teasing the newlyweds

Whenever Luo Jingqing became particularly importunate in his questions, my big brother acted as our buffer and deflected the comments, and we survived our ordeal unscathed.

In the reception room outside the bridal chamber, four of my friends from middle school were merrily playing mahjong, a game they planned to keep up all night.

As night fell, the joshing and joking in our bedroom came to an end. My parents-in-law returned to the Jiangxi Grand Hotel, and Meitang remained at Chenjia Bridge, her new home. Her brother, eight-year-old Aitang, cried and screamed at being parted from his big sister. He wanted to stay with us. It took a lot of people a long time to calm him down and take him away.

他不肯回旅社

The little boy did not want to go back to the hotel.

The day after the wedding, Meitang's family was leaving for Linchuan, so Meitang and I were up early to see them off. A few days later, my aunt called Meitang and me, and my younger brother and his wife, Lizhen, into a small room and took out two packages. She told us that these were bequests from my mother, that she had been their guardian for too long, and now that we were all settled down and had our own families, she could formally hand them over to us. Altogether there was a jin of gold, about a pound in weight, which my brother and I divided in half. There were also two chests of clothes.

Meitang believed we would not be staying long in Nanchang, so she chose only a gown. It was new, of light green brocade lined with snowy white lamb's fleece, the wool more than an inch long. Lizhen took the remainder. There was also a small white cotton wrapper that contained every poem my mother had written in her life, as well as some I had copied out for her. She had wrapped them all carefully and tied the bundle, gift style, with a blue ribbon at one corner. I put the bundle in the clothes chest because we had too many suitcases, and sent the chest back to Nancheng, in the belief that that was our old home so it would be safest there. We had no idea that, sadly, we would never again get the opportunity to go to Nancheng together. Not a single line of my mother's poems survived the turmoil of the years that followed, something that I regret to this day.

姨婶将母亲的遗物分给美棠和丽珍

My aunt presents Meitang and Lizhen with some things my mother had left.

A poem by Ouyang Xiu, "Waves Wash the Sand," goes: "Our time together is so fleeting, my heart is full of infinite regret."[17] In 2008 I went back to the Jiangxi Grand Hotel on my own. The building is now the Nanchang Uprising Museum, because it was here that the first shot was fired in the 1927 uprising. The layout of the hotel has changed too: the spacious, open hall has become a square, closed-off hall in the Chinese style. The shrubs and trees outside are still there, but the tiers of houseplants and flowers inside have gone, and the glass roof has been replaced too. Only the sunlit entrance is the same as when "in bygone years, we journeyed here side by side," as Ouyang's poem puts it.

For ordinary people like us, life is made up of numbers of small details that stay with us for no particular reason and, with the passing of time, turn into treasured memories.

4
Journeying Side by Side

XUZHOU

In the ninth lunar month of 1948 (that is, October), news came that Wang Huiwu's troops had been routed in Jinan but the 83rd Division was still in Xuzhou. Meitang and I decided to go and see what was happening.

That day, we got up just after four o'clock in the morning and prepared the two suitcases we were taking. My father and aunt got up too, to see us off. My father and I sat in the living room in old-fashioned folding chairs, talking about family members who had passed on, until daybreak. Then Meitang and I said goodbye and set out with my orderly, Chen Xusheng.

In Xuzhou, which was looking rather depressed in those days, Meitang and I sometimes went out for a stroll, leaving Chen Xusheng standing guard over the luggage in the hotel. One day we came back to find Chen distraught. Meitang questioned him, and it transpired that he had saved a bit of money and bought a gold ring, but with no safe place to keep it, he had been carrying it in his pocket, wrapped in a kerchief. Now he told us that somehow it had dropped out. Meitang was so sorry for him that she gave him one of her own rings of about the same size, and he cheered up.

在徐州"空军俱乐部"听唱歌

Listening to the singing in the Xuzhou Air Force Club

One day when Meitang and I were out walking, we happened to bump into an old army pal of mine, Zhao Jiuru. He invited us home for a meal. It was a simple meal of noodles and side dishes prepared by his wife, but delicious. They told us about an Air Force Club in Xuzhou that was open to the general public, and Meitang and I went there that evening. It was a Western-style residence converted into a dance hall; customers went in through a narrow back entrance, along three meters of passageway, with the toilets on the left side, and into the dance hall—actually just two rooms knocked into one.

The dance hall had a dozen round tables, a stage against one wall with a microphone, a band, and, in the front, a small dance floor. These were quiet times and there were few guests. Meitang and I found seats at the back and sat there sipping our tea, listening to the singer and watching the dancers.

美棠急喊："那个包是我的！"

Meitang gave a frantic cry: "That bag's mine!"

A couple of hours passed and the entertainment was over. The lights dimmed and the club began to empty. Meitang said she was going to the toilet, and I went to wait for her at the exit. As two of the air force officers were going along the corridor, I suddenly heard them shout in unison:

"Hah! Here's a woman's handbag!" From inside the toilet Meitang heard too and immediately thought of her favorite cream leather handbag, which she had left hanging over the back of the chair. She rushed out, with an anxious cry of "That bag's mine!" The officers handed the bag back to her and stalked off. They had no idea that the bag held more than half a pound of jewelry. If the bag had really gone missing, we would have been in considerable trouble.

We left the club, still upset, and walked along the street for twenty meters or so to the corner in near silence. There, under a dim street-lamp, a vendor was selling pears. Without further ado, we headed over to him and bought two large pears. Then we stood in the street and ate them to celebrate our narrow escape. The pears were ripe and sweet, the sweetest and freshest I have ever eaten.

徐州的油条令我们怀念久之

For a long time, we had fond memories of Xuzhou youtiao.

On the subject of food, Xuzhou's youtiao, or fried breadsticks, were delicious too, tasty and crisp. When we got to Shanghai, Meitang and I sampled all sorts of youtiao, but they were never as good.

A few days passed, and I learned that Wu Lunlun, commander of the 3rd Company, 63rd Brigade, was stationed at Donghecun village outside Xuzhou, and went with Meitang to pay him a visit. As the battle raged closer, most of the villagers had fled to safety, and the place felt desolate. Our visit was just in time, as the 3rd Company was leaving the next morning. We shared their final evening meal, in the modest hall of the company barracks.

少見多怪

A startling sight

I contributed a pressed salted duck, and Wu Lunlun prepared a large number of dishes. After dinner, Meitang and I strolled around the village with Wu and his wife. She was a simple village woman, and the sight of Meitang holding my arm as we walked made her turn to Wu and giggle. Wu admonished her sternly: "What are you giggling about? You really are a country girl. . . ." That night, Meitang shared the bed with her, while Wu Lunlun and I talked until very late.

美棠第一次动手做肉圆子

The first time Meitang made meatballs

Wu was anxious about their impending departure. He told me how he had given his wife a gold bracelet, how he wanted to get her behind the front lines, and so on.

After the 3rd Company left, Meitang and I stayed on awhile, still hoping for news, or to meet friends. Meitang began to learn how to cook. The locals in Xuzhou used to eat pancakes, and one day I asked Chen to buy a stack, and a jin of pork too. Meitang washed the meat well, then put it on the chopping board and began to chop it. She chopped and chopped until it was fine enough to make meatballs. When they were ready, I tasted one. There was something wrong with it—I kept finding little hard bits in the meat. We finally got to the bottom of the mystery— she had chopped the pork skin into the mixture. She grumbled: "Chopping pork skin is such hard work! The only way was to slice it into tiny pieces, and it took a lot of effort!"

And so a few more days passed, but there was no more information to be had, and no more old friends turned up either. The situation was getting increasingly tense, however. Meitang did not like it and began to worry. We discussed things and decided we had better go back to Jiangxi. And so one day in the middle of October, we boarded the train and headed south again.

LINCHUAN

We stayed in Nanchang for a while, and Chen Xusheng returned to his home village.

It was around then that Meitang and I had a quarrel. What about? The truth is, I can't remember. I was young and used to having my own way, and I felt she was being unreasonable. In a fit of pique, I hurled a red thermos that was sitting on the table to the floor. The glass lining shattered, and the water went everywhere. Meitang went and lay on the bed in floods of tears. We did not talk to each other for two or three hours, until I went to try to make it up with her and, to my surprise, she burst into giggles. That was the only quarrel that I remember us ever having.

We discussed my future. Meitang wanted me to go and learn how to run a business with her father, who had a bank in Hankou.[18] He was on his own, with no one to help him. But the political situation was uncertain, there was a general mood of anxiety, and business was slack. My father-in-law wrote saying that this was not a good time, and we should wait. If we were bored, he suggested we go live in Linchuan for a while.

And that was what we did. We still had little to do, and, to pass the time, we sometimes dropped by Meitang's old school to see what was going on, and I played a game or two of basketball there.

我和美棠的一次小争吵

Meitang and I quarreled.

Changsheng Private Bank

An uncle and great-uncle of Meitang's were running a Chinese medicine shop, and sometimes they invited the two of us over for a meal.

The shop was called Prolongs Life, and it lived up to the oddity of its name. We ate in the accounts office. Its black-painted floor was solid and smooth as marble. As you went in, the rooms became increasingly dark and silent—the only light filtered through a few translucent tiles in the ceiling. It was as if time stood still here. The dishes were unusual too. We were given large bowls of food heaped into a high pyramid, topped with stir-fried shredded lotus roots cut until they were as fine as human hair. This was apparently a local custom to welcome an honored guest, and the guest had to be extremely careful in picking up the shreds with chopsticks. If a single shred dropped on the tabletop, it was taken to mean that the guest was boorish and uncouth and did not deserve to be so honored.

There is something else I remember about Linchuan: the Nationalist government was by then in a state of paralysis, and the civil authorities were prone to use any excuse to impose levies. They called it "levying taxes," but in fact it was daylight robbery. The money was never sent to the central government but simply went to line their own pockets. One day when we were there, the governor sent some men to my mother-in-law's house to demand a tax payment, and as I was on hand, I disputed this vigorously. Finally, one of them yelled: "Fine! You can come and argue your case at the governor's office!" "Right, I'll do that!" I answered, and jumped up to go. Suddenly, Meitang got up too. "I'm going with you," she said calmly. On the way, she made a point of letting drop information about her father—for instance, that he was a senator in the provincial government.

When we got to the governor's office, we were kept waiting for a long time in a side room while they made implausible excuses for why we could not see the governor. I had no idea what to do, but Meitang stepped in to negotiate. After a certain amount of haggling, the matter was settled with us paying twelve yuan.

"我跟你一起去！"

"I'm going with you!"

Governor's Office, Zhouxueling, Linchuan county

We stayed about a month in Linchuan, and then Meitang and I went back to the house at Chenjia Bridge. Every day passed with nothing to do, except to play suoha (five-card stud poker) with our friends. It was all good fun, whether you won or lost. We had no idea what the future held, but at least these card games provided us with a great deal of amusement.

OPPOSITE

TOP When we played suoha, we put the bottom card on top of the card just dealt and slowly moved them apart. When the moment came to look at the cards, one was full of anticipation. It was a moment of great excitement.

BOTTOM Spring Festival, 1948. Playing a riotous game of suoha at Uncle Lu's house with family and friends

Clockwise from left: Uncle Lu, Lizhen, Shouru, my father, my aunt, Xili, Li Zhouguo, Mrs. Xiao, Meitang, Pingru, Zhao Chunlin

玩梭哈时，底牌置于发来之牌上面，徐徐移开。看牌立际心中充满期待，极为兴奋之一刹那

一九四八年春节期间在禄母舅房同内与众亲友欢乐地大玩梭哈。

丽珍　寿如　弋亲　姨姐　细俚

禄母舅　　　　　　　　　李胃郭

赵椿林　平如　美棠　萧太太

ZHANGSHU TOWNSHIP

In 1949, Meitang and I decided to make another move—this time to Guizhou province.

We would go and look up Luo Ying. Luo Ying was an expert in bridge construction, chief engineer for the Qiantang River in Hangzhou. He was now in charge of the 4th Region Highway Project, based in Kunming, Yunnan province. Our families went back a long way; his father and my grandfather were old friends. Luo Ying was my grandfather's student and my father's best friend. His nephew was married to Ding, and so Meitang and I discussed it and decided that, rather than hang around doing nothing in Linchuan, we would go to Guizhou and see if I could get work. Any job would do, so long as it was long-term.

As soon as we had made up our minds, we packed our bags and set out. We took a train from Linchuan's Wenjiazhen Station and arrived at midday in Nanchang, where we hoped to take a connecting train to Zhuzhou in Hunan, and then another train on the Hunan-Guangxi line which would take us through Guangxi province to Guizhou.

FROM LEFT Pingru, Father, Luo Ying, Grandmother

When we got to Nanchang my father sent Zhao Chunlin to help us with the baggage. The train was crowded with people fleeing the battle zone for the safety of the southwest. First Meitang got on and held our seats, then I got on and opened the train toilet window, and Zhao passed the bags through the window. Meitang's blue silk parasol fell down a gap in the toilet floor. She was upset, but only for a short while. At two in the afternoon, the train set off and our journey to Guizhou had begun, albeit in a flurry of confusion.

By that time, the railroads were in chaos too. There was no fixed timetable for the trains or any way of knowing what the next station would be. A few hours later, we arrived in Zhangshu (Camphor Tree) township, and we were told the train was terminating. Apparently, the line ahead was not safe. Everyone got off with a sigh, and Meitang and I found ourselves a bed for the night in an old-fashioned inn. The room was tiny, with just a bed and a table, and a window, through which a shaft of light percolated. We were waited on by a girl of seventeen or eighteen, who came in and swept the floor and filled the thermos with hot water, then left.

Meitang and I stowed our luggage and went out for a stroll. Naturally, a restaurant was to be our first port of call. We saw a rather elegant one, with a sign saying, "Zhangshu Dining Hall" hanging outside. For a small town in Jiangxi, the name sounded modern and interesting. We went in to eat—and discovered that inside it was a work of art: a wooden staircase led upstairs, where the doors and windows were all made of wooden latticework, and panes of glass covered the windows outside to keep the rain and wind out. The dining room partitions were constructed of the same latticework, and everything had a rustic charm. Meitang and I sat in a side room upstairs, and ordered a dish of shredded pork and garlic sprouts, and a bowl of minced chicken soup, two yuan each. The waiters soon arrived with the food, and we were astonished at the gargantuan portions—easily enough to satisfy three or four big men. We gorged ourselves as best we could, but by the end, when we reluctantly declared ourselves defeated, a good half was still left. However, in spite of the terrifying amount of food, it was extremely tasty, and during our enforced stay in Zhangshu township, we were regular customers. We just had to remember to ask the waiter for small portions.

For ordinary people like us, life is made up of numbers of small details that stay with us for no particular reason and, with the passing of time, turn into treasured memories.

    This small-town restaurant was just such a place, and Meitang and I talked about it for many years to come.

    On another day, Meitang and I were out for a stroll when she had a sudden thought. The more she thought about it, the more anxious she became, until we decided to hurry back to the hotel. It turned out that we had forgotten to lock our door, and Meitang was worried about the pair of cloth shoes that she had left on the floor. Her aunt had made them for her as a place to store valuables safely: each contained a secret inner sole, in which a gold bracelet had been laid out flat. To the casual observer the shoes looked no different from ordinary shoes, but if someone went in and moved them, or the girl picked them up when she was sweeping the floor, they would surely guess. We rushed back and pushed open the door. Fortunately, the shoes were still where Meitang had left them.

2008.12.18.平如

I paid daily visits to the station to inquire about when trains would be leaving. Finally, one day we were told that a military train was about to leave, destination Hengyang city in Hunan. I was delighted and rushed back to tell Meitang. We quickly packed, settled the bill, and set off. When we found the train, I went to discuss our trip with the officer in charge, and found to my surprise that he was a communications platoon commander who had at one time been billeted in my father's house at Chenjia Bridge.

He was happy to offer us a ride and showed us to the last carriage, an uncovered wagon carrying army families. There was a score of women, each sitting on her own suitcase. They welcomed us, pulled our suitcases on, and helped us up.

Now that we had found a train, we could relax. Evening was drawing in, and dark clouds gathered, threatening rain. The train would not leave for many hours, because apparently a bridge was being repaired up ahead. I spied a small shop selling hot water at the roadside behind the train. It was only two or three hundred meters away, so I set off with our hot water flask, filled it, paid, and put the handful of change in my pocket.

In those days, ordinary folk were suspicious of paper money and dealt only in silver dollars or jiao (ten-cent coins). I was just thinking with satisfaction that we could do with some ten-cent coins when there was a sudden blast from the train whistle, and the train began to move. Horrified, I raced down the track after it, with my fellow travelers shouting anxiously: "Hurry up! Hurry up!" The train was not moving fast because it had just started, but I was carrying a full flask of boiling water in my left hand and had my right hand clamped over my pocket, which was weighed down with ten-cent coins that swung as I ran and slowed me down considerably. I sped along as fast as I could. At first I gained on the train, but when I was fifty meters away, it picked up speed and I realized I was never going to make it! The gap grew to sixty meters, seventy meters, a hundred meters, and my fellow passengers were going frantic. Of course, I was even more frantic. I ran on for another seven or eight minutes, by which time the train was a hundred and fifty meters distant. Then, for some reason I have never fathomed, the train gave a hoot and halted. I put all my effort into making one final sprint and finally caught up. There was jubilation on board. I hurriedly put the thermos on, but when I tried to clamber up myself, I found that the side rails were too high to get over. The train was going to set off again at any moment, and in my anxiety I suddenly caught sight of a round hole a little bigger than a washbasin in the stout wooden floor of the wagon on the right-hand side. It seemed to have been placed there for me by a beneficent Fate. Without much effort, I squeezed through the hole and up into the wagon. Meitang told me what had been going on: when I was just fifty meters away from the train, everyone relaxed: "That's good, he'll catch up." Then the train sped up and there were frantic shouts of "A-ya! A-ya! He'll never catch it!" Meitang was furious with me. "Why were you so stupid?" she demanded. "If you'd thrown away the coins, you could have run faster!"

The skies opened up and it began to rain. Everyone opened their umbrellas and sat leaning against their suitcases. We could not sleep, and the cases were getting soaked, but we were not too bothered. And so the night passed.

The next day, we arrived in Hengyang. It was morning, the rain had stopped, and the sun shone in a rain-washed sky. We all got off the train and went our separate ways.

Meitang and I found a guesthouse run by a mother and daughter near the station on the banks of the Xiangjiang River among a cluster of village houses. As Meitang unpacked, she discovered that the contents of one particular suitcase, pieces of dress

fabric that she had bought on our travels because she liked the design and colors, were soaked through.

As it happened, behind the house was a little yard, surrounded on three sides by bamboo fencing, so she hung all the fabric over the fences to dry. In the sunshine, it looked quite beautiful. She gave our dirty clothes to the old woman who ran the guesthouse, to get them washed. The laundry charged by the item: jacket and trousers were an item, handkerchief and socks were also an item, and each item cost five cents. We were young and heedless in those days, and did not bother to do the math. Nor did we keep a close eye on the dozens of fabric lengths drying outside. It was not until we were back in Nanchang the following year and wanted to get the fabric made up into clothes that we discovered that three or four of the nicest pieces had disappeared. When we thought back, we figured that it was probably our landlady who had made off with them.

LIUZHOU

The Hunan-Guangxi railroad was still running. Meitang and I stayed just two days in Hengyang and then set off for Liuzhou. We planned to take a break for a few days and do some sightseeing.

Liuzhou and its surroundings were very scenic, and the South China climate was warm and sunny. Meitang and I liked it very much. Every day, we strolled through the town streets, which were flanked by qilou, covered arcades typical of the region. Everyone, young and old, male and female, wore short tunics and trousers, and fanned themselves with big fans. They wore wooden sandals, and the streets were filled with a rhythmic clack-clacking as they walked. There were no vehicles in those days, and pedestrians strolled around as if they had not a care in the world.

Right in the middle of the bustling center of Liuzhou was a small park, full of grotesquely shaped rocks piled one on top of the other to resemble mountains. There were stands selling tea and snacks too. This was in May and the weather was hot. Around four or five in the afternoon, everyone poured out of their houses to enjoy the cooler air. Meitang and I ambled along after the crowds, and always ended up at this little park. We would find a couple of seats on the rocky slopes, where we would sip our tea and enjoy the fresh air and the scenery.

We were greatly impressed by a local dish called "teeming fishes congee," though we had no idea how it had acquired the character 牲 (teeming) in its name. You could get it in snack stalls and eateries all over Liuzhou.

數日後由衡陽乘
火車至柳州，在此
又休息約一周。
時值初夏，街上
行人皆短衣、短褲，
木屐。街道旁有一
假山堆砌之公園，
處處堆砌之公園，
處飲茶乘涼享
受南國夏季
風光。街上無公交
車，無自行車，無
警察，乃真正的
步行街也。

A few days later, we boarded the train from Hengyang to Liuzhou, where we had a weeklong break.
It was early summer in Liuzhou, and everyone wore tunics and short trousers, and wooden sandals.
There was plenty of cool shade in this park, which was full of rocks piled one on top of the other to
resemble mountains. Meitang and I went there to drink our tea and enjoy the southern summer.
There was no public transportation, or bicycles, or police, so these were genuine "pedestrian zones."

There were places selling teeming fishes congee everywhere.

To the right of the entrance, there was always a bubbling vat of hot congee, of just the right consistency, not too thick or too runny, and very flavorful. On the left, a large rectangular tray sat on a table, laden with deboned fish fillets, pigs' livers, and pigs' hearts, all thinly sliced. There were almost a hundred choices, but the fish slices were always the favorites. The congee was served like this: first, fish slices were laid in the bottom of the bowl, then hot congee was ladled over them, then condiments were added, and chopped scallions, ginger, or chili pepper sprinkled on top. The whole was mixed together so that the delicately sliced fish cooked in the rice, and then it was ready to serve. We loved to watch the drama around the cooking, and we loved the way the fresh, hot congee slipped down our throats.

It was often said that one should "die in Liuzhou"[19] because Liuzhou was famous for its coffins. We took it into our heads to investigate the coffin makers but never found a single business, probably because they were outside the city center. We spent a week or so there, then boarded a train to Guiyang city. When I got to the ticket office to buy our tickets, I discovered that two tickets cost sixty silver dollars. Paper currency was no longer accepted, and I handed a great pile of silver coins through the window.

GUIYANG

We happened to arrive in Guiyang right in the middle of the Dragon Boat Festival.

At noon, Meitang and I walked to the so-called Main Crossroads, actually just a cross-roads in the center of the city. There were few people around, and the shops on either side of the street all looked much the same. I wanted to buy some zongzi, sticky rice dumplings steamed in leaves, because it was traditional to eat them at the Dragon Boat Festival, but could find nowhere that sold them. Finally, I saw one old lady sitting on the sidewalk, with a basket at her side packed with homemade zongzi, and bought three or four to share with Meitang. They were quite different from our lye zongzi and had little flavor, but at least they were festive.

That night, we stayed at the Brazil Hotel, the biggest in Guiyang. This was a two-story brick and timber building, with a little courtyard on the left as you entered. The guest rooms were ranged around the courtyard, downstairs and upstairs. The better rooms were square, with a big window overlooking the courtyard, and cost fifty cents. However, they were all taken, and we were given a room on the ground floor next to the stairs. The staircase took a chunk out of the room, making it asymmetrical, so we got a discount, and paid only forty cents. Meitang and I were rather annoyed, and we argued with the receptionist. Why couldn't we have a proper square room?

We were told that we could swap rooms only if someone checked out the next day, and that was that. It seems ridiculous, looking back on it, that we were so set on having a square room. It was not as if we were staying long. But we were young back then.

The next day, we did indeed get another room, upstairs, square-shaped, and facing the entrance. So we were happy.

2009.10.27. 平如

2009.10.27.平如

I then wrote to Ding's husband in Anshun city, telling him our address. He wrote back, saying that he would send a car for us. We were content to explore the town while we waited.

There was a large number of restaurants, the top ones being the Guansheng Garden, the Three Coins, and the Big Shanghai. The Guansheng Garden was never crowded, and Meitang and I liked to go there for morning tea and Cantonese-style sweet and savory midmorning snacks—chashao pork buns, zongzi, paper-bag chicken, and sticky rice chicken.

Each saucerful cost around thirty cents, and we loved the intense flavors. One day we had finished eating but had not yet left when a well-dressed man in his forties, with the air of a businessman, suddenly paused near our table and smiled at us. Judging by his accent, he was probably from Jiangsu or Zhejiang province. He asked where we were from and what we were doing, nodding and smiling and full of bonhomie. We got the impression he had left home far behind to come to this southern paradise, as yet untouched by war, in search of peace and freedom.

We were warm and generous in those days. In the Brazil Hotel, we met a couple even younger than we were who had run out of money and were stuck there awaiting a remittance from home. The weather was rather hot, but we had a wooden balcony outside our room with a rectangular table and benches. Meitang used to put out fruit and snacks, pumpkin seeds, peanuts, and the like, and brew some tea, and invite them over to sit and chat with us.

Sometimes we ate in the Big Shanghai or the Three Coins, which were attractively lit with neon illuminations at the entrance. It all looked deceptively peaceful, and we were young enough to take it at face value. We had no idea of the dramas that were about to unfold.

More than two weeks passed. One day I was reading at our upstairs window when I saw a middle-aged man, plainly dressed like a government functionary, walking into the hotel. Intuition told me that this was the man my brother-in-law had sent. And so it was. He was head of the Guiyang Section of the Highway Department and said he had been sent by Superintendent Luo. The trouble was that the official car had broken down. The only way he could help was to take us to the long-distance bus station in a pony and cart. The next day, he picked us up and took us there. We said goodbye to him and got on the bus to our destination, Anshun city, the last leg of a very long journey.

ANSHUN

My sister Ding and her husband lived in the housing provided for the section's officials and their families. Their house was timber-built and looked more like a temple or an old-style *yamen* than like a residence. Inside the entrance there was a large courtyard with covered walkways on both sides. The buildings were rather dark, and had an ancient, peaceful feel.

In Anshun we lived collectively, each contributing four yuan a month for food. The section cook, Zhang Shanqing, provided three meals a day for everyone: congee for breakfast, and six dishes with soup for lunch and dinner. We ate mostly pork and beef. We were on a plateau, with few lakes or ponds. Ding had been fond of fish at home, but she could not get any here.

Our Strange Room

The room Meitang and I moved into was most unusual. It was on the second floor and hexagonal in shape, like a pavilion but boxed in. It was twenty or thirty square meters and had windows on all sides but no door. You entered the room by a stepladder and a trapdoor about seventy or eighty centimeters square in the floor, like a theater trapdoor through which a martial arts hero might pop up at any minute. There was a wooden bed, no other furniture at all. We used it only for sleeping and spent most of the day downstairs. I loved this strange hideaway. When the moon was full, we slept with the windows open, and moonlight poured over the bed.

I could recite with true feeling the famous Li Bai poem: "Before my bed the bright moon shines, / Looking like frost on the ground. / I look up, at the bright moon, / I look down, and think of home."[20]

When the weather turned stormy, however, the windows on all sides would clatter and shake, and you actually felt it physically, just like the line from Xu Hun's poem: "A storm is brewing, wind fills the tower."[21] Those who live in urban reinforced concrete homes can have no idea of the beauty of these mountains, and the painterly and poetic feelings they can inspire.

2008.7.6. 平如

奇妙的「房間」

美棠和我的住处为一个二楼的
六角亭,四面有窗,除一床外,别
无他物,地板一角装有一块盖板,
乘梯上楼后可将此板盖上。环境
奇佳。一切活动都在楼下。

每逢月明如水之夜,开窗而眠,
则月光洒满床前,李白之佳句:
「床前明月光,疑是地上霜」便目
然会联想入于脑际。

又当风雨交加,电闪雷鸣之际,则在
风大作,四面窗子劈拍作响,東里更
动,便能亲身体会「山雨欲来风
满楼」之情怀,此和山開野趣、画
意诗情,绝非大城市中住钢筋水
泥房屋之人们试能领略得到
的也。

平如谨 二〇〇九年
一月二十九日

We waited for a while in Anshun, but there was no word from Kunming or my brother-in-law's uncle Luo Ying. We discovered later that things were not going well there. Luo Ying had moved to a new job and was no longer in the 4th Region Highway Project, so there was nothing he could do to get me work. However, my brother-in-law pulled strings and managed to get me taken on as an employee in Anshun by using the quotas of two highway maintenance teams. The work did not pay much, but at least I had something to do. Every morning after breakfast, at about eight o'clock, two pony carts came to take us to work. The ponies ambled along Anshun's single main street until, as the houses thinned out and the mountains loomed around us, we arrived at the section headquarters. Zhang Shanqing delivered our lunches to us, and, at three in the afternoon, the pony carts turned up again to take us home.

We arrived home around four, and Ding would round everyone up to set the table for a game of mahjong. She was a smart woman, with astonishing powers of reasoning, memory, and strategic planning. She had no interest in cooking and fashion, or in housework, and she had little social life in this remote area, so all her intellectual energies were poured into mahjong. She hardly ever lost money. The other players were myself, Wu the accountant, and Zhao the cashier. Wu always used to announce as he turned up: "Mrs. Luo! We've come to give you money!"

Things were not good, because Luo Ying had changed jobs. My brother-in-law managed to get me taken on as an "employee," by using the quotas of two highway maintenance teams, so that I went to work with all the other staff housed alongside us. It was undemanding, just a way of passing the time.

Anshun had no supermarkets, or cinemas, or karaoke . . . the only entertainment was to play mahjong with Ding, Wu the accountant, and Zhao the cashier. Ding was extremely good at mahjong and always won.

We were allowed to use the communal dining room, and we always ate our meals with Ding and her family. In the evenings, other members of the staff took turns inviting us for hot pot. Fifty cents could buy a pig's head and greens and bean curd, and we washed them down with mao-tai liquor. We would ask Zhang Shanqing to prepare the ingredients for us and pass a most pleasant evening together.

时机恰巧，罗英
此时已卸任二姐
乃设法以两个
道班（工人）名
额，让我担任
只雇员工邮员
随同他们职员
一起上班工作
甚简。暂混
时光而已。

安顺无电影院、
无公园、无夏贺
商店……唯一娱
乐乃是与定姐、
老赵打麻将而
已。定姐精通
会计若吴、出纳
此首、穗是
赢家。

老吴　定姐　美棠　老赵　平如

2009年
元月16日
平如畫

集体食堂伙食可自愿参加。定姐
一家与我们均吃大伙，晚间我们与一些
相熟职工轮流请客。五角钱，河头一只
大猪头，再买些蔬菜、豆腐，畅饮棻
台酒，叫厨师张善清备办。其乐融。

美棠　平如

2009年
元月16日
平如畫

In actual fact, Zhang and Zhao were not bad players, just not as good as Ding. The real rookie was me—I knew only a few simple rules, and I was always going to lose every game. I found myself copies of manuals like *Tips for Success at Mahjong* and *How to Play Mahjong* at a pavement bookstall and did my homework, but unfortunately all that writing about war was not the same thing as a real battle. Sometimes Meitang could not bear to see me losing and would join the fray, but she was not much better than I was, and we lost just the same.

Once we had finished our game, what were we to do next? We had another way of amusing ourselves: making a hot pot.

Wu, Zhao, Li, Yang, Yu, and myself all took turns being hosts. We gave the money to Zhang Shanqing and asked him to prepare everything. By evening, he would have a large pot of broth ready. It was placed on top of a charcoal burner in the center of a round table, and the table was set with dishes of green vegetables, bean curd, soybean paste, and sesame oil, and a large plate of thinly sliced meat from the pig's head. We had several bottles of liquor brought too and sat around enjoying the hot pot—cooking the meat and vegetables in the broth, seasoning it in the dips—drinking and chatting. Those of us who knew Peking operas sang a few songs, and it was all good fun. Meitang was never absent; she loved a good party. She never drank alcohol, but she ate the food, especially enjoying the pig's head, drank a little broth, and listened as we talked nonsense.

Apart from that, it was easy enough to make friends if you liked basketball. A young man named Li, the general manager, and I got to know each other well through basketball, and we often went to play on a nearby primary school's courts. The head of one of the subsections, Yang, had contacts with the middle school nearby and told us that they wanted to play a friendly game with our section team. Yang and Li and I formed the core of the team, and we recruited another two who knew a bit about basketball and went and played against the middle school team. Those young students did not stand a chance against us.

"韭菜合子"真好吃

The garlic-chive pies were delicious.

Yang was very hospitable. Once, he invited my sister and her husband, Meitang and myself, to his house for a meal of garlic-chive pies. It turned out that the family was from the northeast, and he and his wife and mother were experts at making them. They got the seasoning and the texture and the pan heat just right. The pies were a tour de force, and we gorged ourselves. For a long time afterward, Meitang and I reminisced about those garlic-chive pies. I had the temerity to try to make them myself a few times, but they were a complete failure.

2009. 1. 16 平如

此洞洞口果是高大,有如現今可希尔顿已五星级宾馆之接待大厅。由向导(即今之导遊)执火把率我们鱼貫而入.洞湻约五百米.此无非是钟乳石与水潭那构成的各类奇观而已。

郡旦有一名胜已——黄龙洞.某次段上去查修桥梁,大家乃乘公車(去逛)因坍桥与洞相距甚近之故。

Yellow Dragon Cave (Huang Long Dong) was a famous local beauty spot. On one occasion, when the section engineers were sent to inspect a nearby damaged bridge, we got a ride on their "bus" and went sightseeing. The entrance to the cave soared upward like the entrance hall of the present-day Hilton Hotel. The guide led us in, holding the bamboo-stick torch aloft. The cave was five hundred meters deep and filled with impressive stalactites and pools of water.

One day, a bridge in one of the subsections suffered damage, and the section head-quarters had to dispatch an engineer to inspect it and draw up a plan for repair. It was a long road trip away, and someone said that there were sights to see—Yellow Dragon Mountain and, on the mountain, Yellow Dragon Cave. The superintendent felt there was no time to lose; everyone boarded the truck, and Ding, Meitang, and I went with them. The truck was a real classic model. As soon as the engine fired up, it shook all over, and the mudguards flapped so hard they looked like a fly's wings. In the back of the truck there were benches with paint flaking off down each side. The women sat there, while the men stood in the middle. Meitang and Ding got special treatment—they had seats in the driver's cab. And so, lurching and shuddering, the truck moved off.

At Yellow Dragon Cave, our guide lit some torches he had brought with him, bundles of bamboo sticks bound together and dipped in something that looked like tar. Back then, Yellow Dragon Cave was completely undeveloped. The stones were slippery underfoot, and the path meandered past puddles and pools filled with dark green water. The darkness of the cave threatened to swallow up the light from our torches, while water emerged from somewhere above our heads and trickled down the stone walls, making a tinkling sound. We were young back then, and Meitang had no trouble in keeping up with us as we blundered along, over stones and through the shoals. The guide pointed to this or that rock feature: "That's a bodhisattva. . . . This is a frog. . . ." But they did not look much like his descriptions and we paid little attention. Then he told us a story. The previous year, a young couple from another province had asked for a guide to the cave. When they got to the deepest part of the cave, the guide killed them, robbed them, and vanished without a trace. He left the corpses in the cave, and they were not found until another sightseeing group passed by several months later. Meitang and I were horrified at the story. By then, we had reached the farthest point. Up ahead was just a wet wall, and everyone retraced their steps.

2008.7.6. 平女口 平

安顺山区苗族人民甚多,民
风淳朴,生活艰苦,每隔十天半
月会来赶集,他们带来家产
品换取一些日用品或银钱。某日,
美棠与我去赶集游玩,我见一
中年妇女在卖板栗,我未向价就
说:"买五角钱的。"不料她用一个大
撮斗四满上地装了一斗给我,我手足
无措,只好脱下上装,兜着走吧。
平

A great many people of Miao nationality lived
in the mountains around Anshun. They were
simple folk. Every couple of weeks, they made
the trip down to Anshun to hold a market,
bringing their products to exchange for cash
or daily necessities. One day, Meitang and I
were strolling around the market and I saw a
middle-aged woman selling chestnuts. I did not
ask the price and just said: "Fifty cents' worth,
please." To my astonishment, she grabbed a
round-bottomed basket, filled it to the brim
with chestnuts, and gave it to me. I had nothing
to carry them in so finally I took off my jacket,
spread it on my knees, poured the chestnuts
in, and bundled them up. I certainly had not
bargained for that many.

The markets were lively affairs, and Meitang and I always went along to see the fun. The Miao, men and women alike, traveled sometimes dozens of li over the mountains, carrying farm products and handicrafts to sell: there were chickens, eggs, sweet corn, sweet potatoes, and beans; hand towels, head towels, and aprons. With the cash they earned, the Miao bought articles of daily use, such as matches, kerosene, and soap, then went back home. Their lives were extremely hard. They all dressed in blue outfits, embroidered with intricate designs, and wore turbans of blue cloth wrapped around their heads. They were simple folk, and mixing with them was like going back to a society of several hundred years ago.

Apart from that trip, Meitang and I spent most of the time walking and eating snacks. The main street in Anshun ran from east to west. One day we came upon a noodle restaurant called Eight Hundred Springtimes. Was it really telling us that the establishment was eight hundred years old? We were skeptical, but it was such an elegant name that we thought we might as well give it a try. It was a dilapidated, dirty place with a narrow front and a stove at the entrance; a couple of rickety, unpainted tables; and three or four rough wooden benches. The walls were black with grime, and, in the back, I could see heaps of broken windows and bits of copper and scrap iron. The back window was covered with cobwebs that fluttered in the breeze.

The Anshun streets were narrow. West Street had a small restaurant selling rice noodles and a sign that read "Eight Hundred Springtimes." It was a dilapidated, dirty place with shabby old furniture, but Meitang and I decided to give the noodles a try. They were at least as good as Nancheng noodles, and not expensive, so we became regulars. But there were few other customers, and the owner was not making much of a living.

安顺街道窄小。西街有一米
粉店，招牌叫"八佰春"。店
堂破旧，两张桌子也系旧物，
环境甚差。美棠与我试
吃其米粉，味道不逊于南城
之米粉，乃常去光顾。价
亦不贵。但顾客稀少，生
活水平所限也。

Meitang and I were not particularly bothered about that; as Jiangxi folk, we liked our soup noodles, and, since we were here, we felt we had to compare Guizhou noodles with our Jiangxi version. We sat opposite each other, and two bowls were brought to the table. The noodles were tender and slippery, and compared favorably with our Magu noodles. The broth was fresh-tasting and came topped with finely ground stir-fried pork, tiny deep-fried cubes of pork fat, and a sprinkling of shredded scallions and ginger. The scallions were a brilliant green, and the tasty meat contrasted with the bland, clear broth. We loved the noodles and became regulars. The odd thing was that we two were almost the only customers. We never saw any locals eating there. Perhaps the shopfront was too bare for them, or perhaps the price was too high for the locals. But every time Meitang and I talked about this "eight-hundred-year-old" noodle restaurant, we exchanged delighted smiles. I wonder if it is still there.

There was one snack that all the Anshun locals loved to eat: roasted corncobs. The Miao people sold these—they set up their stoves by the side of the road, and the corncobs cooked slowly over the fire. They were chewy and tasty and very cheap, our favorite between-meals snack.

贵州安顺的"零食"

Snacks in Anshun, Guizhou province

贵州安顺赏月图

Moongazing in Anshun, Guizhou province

In no time at all, the Midautumn Festival was upon us. After our evening meal, I bought two Cantonese-style mooncakes from a street vendor and took them back to our "pavilion room." Meitang and I lay on the bed, eating our mooncakes and wondering how our families were doing. On all sides, the moonlight poured in through the windows and lit up an expanse of floor. It was 1949, the last Midautumn Festival of the old society.

安顺街上有个算命先生名叫"卓龙年"。
卓先生排八字灵验。某日，美棠与我即
去找他，此人收费不便宜，要现洋四元。我安
上我的生辰八字。他讲了很多现已不复记忆，
只记得有一句"平生利于东南"。此语在
我以后的生命历程中证明极其正确。

一九四九年十二月初，安顺解放。
军代表接管了公路段。半月后，
如夫及厚荣所有职工奉命迁往贵
阳。我坐车最后一辆货车的行李堆上，
看到即将离开的安顺城庙屋宇，心中
想道："这个地方今后恐怕永远不会再
来了！"

2009.10.20. 平如

TOP There was a fortune-teller in Anshun by the name of Zhuo the Deaf. His predictions were supposed to be very accurate, and one day Meitang and I went to see him. His prices were high, at four silver dollars. I gave him my birth data, and he gave me a long spiel. I have forgotten most of what he said, but I do remember one sentence: "The southeast will always be good for you." As the future course of my life was to prove, this was exactly right.

BOTTOM At the beginning of December 1949, Anshun was liberated. The military took over control of the Highway Department section office, and two weeks later, Ding's husband and all of us employees were transferred to Guiyang city. I sat on a pile of luggage in the very last truck, gazing at the buildings of Anshun and thinking: We'll probably never come back to Anshun again!

By November, rumors were rife. Meitang and I went to see Zhuo the Deaf, a fortune-teller. His shopfront was modest, only half the width of normal shops. He was a short man, with a bony face. The fee was quite high, four silver dollars. His message—"The southeast will always be good for you"—stuck in my mind. Meitang and I were already discussing leaving because I was not a permanent employee and we were unlikely to be able to stay long-term, so the old man's words reinforced our inclination to leave.

The Kuomintang Nationalist troops in the region had retreated in early December. Now there was a power vacuum in Anshun. The gentry and merchants raised money and paid local gangsters to maintain law and order. In our compound, we were on high alert. The main gate was kept locked and barred all day, and we did not dare sleep too soundly at night. Two or three days later, one sunny, cloudless winter's day, the People's Liberation Army entered Anshun. The streets were lined with people waving red and green streamers and welcoming placards. And so Anshun was liberated.

Not long afterward, the new government relocated the entire Highway Department section, lock, stock, and barrel, to Guiyang. When we arrived, we were all accommodated in an old courtyard-style mansion. The meals were altogether different from before: a large iron cooking pot was set on a table and a charcoal burner placed underneath. The pot was filled with beef, greens, and bean curd, and a heap of chili paste was put on one side. However, we were all tense and anxious—we had no idea what was to happen to us.

2008.7.6.平如

One day I was out walking when I suddenly saw a sign in front of a shop which read, in big red letters: "Leaving for Nanchang," with "Nanchang" written especially large. This was a wonderful surprise, and I rushed over to inquire. It transpired that a Mr. Xin, who was from Nanchang, owned a U.S.-made Dodge bus and was departing the next day for Hunan, destination Nanchang. He was looking for passengers. The fare was sixty dollars per person. Then and there, I paid a deposit and rushed back to tell Meitang. She was delighted too, and without delay we packed our bags. Ding and her husband were astonished at our sudden departure. That evening, under the lamplight, my brother-in-law hurriedly wrote some letters to my father, and Ding got out half a jin of dried snow fungus for us to take as a gift.

As we were about to set off the next day, I asked Mr. Xin whether Meitang could sit in the driver's cabin, and he agreed. Meitang was anxious to keep her gold jewelry safe. He said he knew what to do. When we had wrapped it up, he put the bundle inside one

車輪
制动
三角木

美常將武帶金飾
老辛置于汽車輪胎中以
策安全；而老辛亦將其可秘
密口相告，木制之制动器路
（左图）中藏有鵶片、田南
昌后可赚一筆也。

2008.7.6.于如

Triangular wooden brake chock

Meitang gave her jewelry to Mr. Xin to stow away safely in the bus tire. He, in turn,
let us in on a secret: in the wooden brake chock, he had hidden
opium that he was planning to sell for a profit in Nanchang.

of the bus tires, where it would be perfectly safe. Then he confided to us that his bus had a triangular-shaped wooden brake chock, which, when placed behind the wheel of the stationary bus, prevented it from moving. There was a thriving opium trade in Guizhou, and Mr. Xin had done a deal and acquired some. Then he had hollowed out the brake chock and hidden the opium inside. The chock looked like a solid piece of wood, so it was the perfect hiding place. It was kept under the seat and would certainly escape detection.

The Xuefeng mountain range on the borders of western Hunan and Guizhou provinces had been bandit country from ancient times. After we set off, I discovered that the area we were traveling through was still lawless, and the road by no means safe. Every now and then I would lift the canvas that covered the back of the bus and watch our lurching progress along the mountain roads, above deep ravines, at the bottom of which the wrecks of vehicles were clearly visible.

2008. 7. 6 千知

Xin liked to put his foot on the gas and had frightening confidence in his driving skills. Liu, the assistant driver, was a much steadier hand at the wheel. They took turns driving, making the best time possible and stopping only for midday meals and overnight. One evening, over dinner at an inn, we heard some news: a bus in front of us had been robbed, and so had the bus coming behind. We had escaped by some lucky fluke, but Meitang and I were extremely worried. We went back to our room, sat on the edge of the bed warming our hands over the brazier, and talked things over. We considered the dangers of the road ahead, and it occurred to us to go back. I went to tell Xin that we did not want to go any farther and asked if he could refund us some of our fare, but he was reluctant to do this and urged us to continue our journey. At that point, I went back to the room to talk to Meitang. We could see how difficult it would be to retrace our steps, and we made a joint decision: we would take a gamble and go on.

The next evening, Meitang and I burned all the photographs of me wearing my Kuomintang Nationalist military uniform in the brazier. I also had a green utility uniform, which we decided it was best not to take with us, so we discarded that too.

Four days later, we arrived safe and sound at Number 18, Chenjia Bridge, Nanchang city. It was December 1949.

Meitang and I saw so many families being
wrenched apart by quarrels and by destitution.
Fortunately, it never entered our heads to split up.

5

Crossroads

When we got home, my father registered us for our *hukou,* residents' permits, and I went to the local police station to fill out the Demobilized Officer Registration Form.[22] The political situation was daily growing more tense. My father-in-law closed his bank in Hankou, and, before going home to Linchuan, stopped off in Nanchang city.

At Spring Festival that year, we all gathered around the table for our usual games. But once the festivities were over, I had to consider how I would earn a living. My father-in-law was also thinking about what to do. He came to Nanchang to discuss matters with my father, and it was decided that he and I should open a shop. But what kind of shop? We liked the idea of making products, rather than having a purely retail business. Why not make noodles? We would buy the flour and produce the noodles like true artisans.

With the nature of our business agreed upon, we needed a name. At first my father-in-law suggested Noodles for the Multitudes, but after my father convinced him the character for "Multitudes," 羣, was too complex, he suggested, 民, "Noodles for the People" instead.

I thought we should rent somewhere small, sell dried noodles, and see how that went, but my father-in-law had bigger plans and found a large, recently constructed shop on the corner of Zhushi and Xiangshan South Streets. It was two stories, and there was a small room on the left-hand side downstairs that my father-in-law could move into.

OPPOSITE LEFT **My father-in-law and my father discuss the new business.** OPPOSITE RIGHT **A tale of business in Nanchang.**

In December 1949, the two of us returned to Number 18, Chenjia Bridge, Nanchang city. I was then twenty-eight and Meitang was twenty-five.

The political situation was growing daily more tense, and my father-in-law closed his private bank in Hankou, and went home to Linchuan.

At the beginning of 1950, my father-in-law arrived in Nanchang city and began to discuss with my father opening a business for the two of us to run. We felt that just running a shop would be difficult and preferred the idea of something that involved some physical labor. Why not open a noodle shop, in other words, a small artisan business? At least it was better than sitting idly at home.

He wanted to call it Noodles for the Multitudes, but my father thought the character for "Multitudes," 羣, was too complicated for people to read, so he suggested using 民, so that it read "Noodles for the People" instead.

My father-in-law went out every day to look for premises. He was used to running big businesses, and had big ideas. He found a large, newly built shop on the corner of Zhushi and Xiangshan South streets. It had two floors, each around thirty square meters, and a yard behind it. The rent was four stones' weight of rice per month (in those days, payments were generally made with goods, not money). My father-in-law got a friend of his in Hankou to buy a noodle-cutting machine, we applied for a business license, and I stamped the wrapping paper with my own design. My father's secretary, Zhao Chunlin, who was having trouble making ends meet, came to work in the shop. We bought the flour ... and within three months we were open for business!

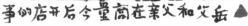
▲岳父和亲家在商量今后开店的事

南昌經商日記

平如
2010.6.4

一九四九年十二月，我俩回到江西南昌陈家桥。认识、筹划又多么不如改为吕昆吕宗，于是决定取名为吕利民面店吕。

岳父自己每日上街去找店面，他做惯了大生意，服界大，在象山南路（珠市街）找到一家新完工的

一九五〇年年初，岳父即来到南昌，他和父亲商议准备和我俩合开一个店铺。考虑到单纯的买卖生意恐怕难做，最好要生产有点劳动力的产品，要么就开个切面店吧，这属于小小的手工业。岳父起初打算把店名取为"利群"，父亲说："利群"二字较难

附周日益紧张，生意不好做，沿沼的岳父也结束了钱庄的业务，回到江西临川。美棠25岁。

铺子门面有三十平方，有两层，后面有一个院子，月租四石米（那时一律以实物计价），岳父托沿沼的朋友一头来请了工商执照，我们买来一架木制面机器，我印一张朱砂面纸，父亲乘的木记赵椿林抄，时无事，我们便也加入面店工作。我们买好面粉……于三月间便便正式开张营业啦

平如

BOTTOM CHARACTERS **Xiangshan South Road.** RIGHT **Zhushi Street.**

I applied for a business license and stamped several hundred sheets of paper for wrapping the noodles with a stamp I had designed myself. The stamp incorporated the noodle shop sign and the address. My father's secretary, Zhao Chunlin, joined us, helping to make noodles and carry water. We gave him board and lodging, but there was no question of wages. He received just fifty cents a month as pocket money. We spent three yuan on a semicircular black-lacquer shop counter. It was rather scruffy, but a glass-fronted bookcase placed on the left against the wall lent an elegant touch. The bookcase had belonged to Mao Yisun, but we now put it to much humbler use, as a place to store the bundles of dried noodles.

Twenty or thirty bags of best-quality Warship Brand flour were piled up at the front of the shop. There was a square table for customers who wanted to eat in the shop, and the noodle cutter stood against the right-hand wall. The kitchen was at the very back. There was a spacious yard, of about fifty or sixty square meters, behind the shop. We put a bamboo fence around it and generally used it for hanging out clothes to dry. And that year at the Midautumn Festival, we also put a small table with fruit and other offerings in the yard and sat there to admire the moon. Meitang and I lived over the shop.

Zhao Chunlin and I visited similar establishments, from which we hoped to learn a few trade secrets by observing how the old hands made their noodles. Then we came back and made repeated experiments. The best that can be said is that we managed to make noodles. The trouble was that they were not of consistent quality, and came out either too wet or too dry.

CLOCKWISE FROM 12:00 Lizhen, my aunt, my father, Shouru, my elder brother's wife, my elder brother, Meitang, Pingru, Zhao Chunlin, my father-in-law

We continued making preparations until March 1950, when we opened for business. By then, Meitang was pregnant. On the first day, my father-in-law was in an ebullient mood, buying all sorts of food and wining and dining a crowd of friends in our new shop.

美棠和我
喜欢的小吃

锅贴水饺

油炸豆腐

Meitang and I enjoyed street snacks.

Guotie pot-sticker dumplings (top); the
sign reads "Pine Crane Garden" (middle);
deep-fried bean curd (bottom).

此时店中的工作大致
分工如下：岳父（买菜、
做饭）平如（做麺外勤、
美棠（照管柜台）岳
椿林（担水、协助做麺）
另请一女佣（朱妈）做
家事。

一九五〇年四月十九日晚
十时许，希曾出生于
麺店的二楼。请一位姓
瓯的助产生接生，左此
前数日，父亲云曾梦
见有一条黑龙在麺店
门前翻腾飞舞。

五月底，为希曾满月之日，我
们在麺店请客。父亲、姨娘、大哥、
三弟、福母舅母、姑、以及我外婆
家的八舅母、十舅母等各家都
来祝贺。店中摆了两桌酒。岳
母也自临川赶来，甚为热闹。

We divided up the work in the shop more or less as follows: my father-in-law did the shopping and cooked, I made the noodles and was the contact for our suppliers, Meitang served at the counter, and Zhao Chunlin fetched water and helped me make the noodles. In addition, we employed a woman, Ma Zhu, to help around the store.

Just past ten in the evening on April 29, 1950, our first baby, Xizeng, was born in our room above the noodle shop. Meitang was attended by a midwife called Mrs. Nie. A few days previously, my father had dreamed that a black dragon was flapping and soaring above the door of the shop.

At the end of May, Xizeng was one month old and we invited the extended family for a celebratory meal: there was my father, my aunt, my elder brother, Third Brother, Uncle Lu (my mother's brother), and my father's sister. There were uncles and aunts from my maternal grandmother's side, and my mother-in-law came from Linchuan too. We set out two tables of food and wine in the store and had a big party.

The shop was filled with the sound of laughter and chatter. I remember it as vividly as if it was yesterday.

One day, when Meitang and I were strolling down Xiangshan South Road, we saw a sign that read "Pine Crane Garden." We looked at it—it was not a restaurant at all, but someone's house; there were only two tables and no other customers in sight. They served guotie, pot-sticker dumplings. Curious, we went in to try them. They were extremely good; the skins were thin and crisp, golden brown without being burned, cooked for just the right amount of time; the filling was tender and juicy; and the prices were reasonable. We started to go there often.

On one corner of the crossroads with Qipan Street, there was a small shop that specialized in deep-fried bean curd. It was very famous. Large chunks of bean curd were deep-fried, then put back in the wok with seasoned broth and simmered for a long time. When they were ready, the pieces were brown outside and tender and white inside. They came steaming hot to the table and were a real delicacy. I often took a bowl there in the evening, and bought four pieces to take home for Meitang and me to snack on.

On April 29, 1950, Meitang went into labor. In the evening, as her labor pains intensified, I rushed for the doctor, and my father and aunt came over to stay with Meitang. Two or three hours later, Xizeng was born in the bedroom above the store. The whole family was overjoyed. The "Xi" in his name means "hope" and was chosen by my father, who said that a few days before, he had dreamed of a black dragon fluttering and swooping over the shop door. The second character, "zeng," is shared by all the cousins of his generation.

麵店生意不佳，每日就只售出二斤濕麵、卷子麵，也很少有人問津。每日售得的錢，連交店租都不夠。

二〇一〇、六、四 平如

2010.12.26. 平如

趙椿林睡於樓下店堂內，不時他都用竹床頂住後門，某一晚，他床未頂住，就在此晚，竊賊推門而入，偷去一袋麵粉，和一把做切面的「中刀」。次日清晨，他岳父起床最早，是他第一個發覺的。

Business in the store was poor: we sold only a few jin of fresh noodles per day. No one was much interested in our bundles of dried noodles either. Our daily income was not enough to cover even the rent.

Zhao Chunlin normally slept in the store, with his bamboo bed against the back door to secure it. But one evening he must have left a gap, and a thief pushed the door open and took a bag of flour and the knife used for cutting the medium-size noodles. It was my father-in-law who discovered the theft when he got up early the next morning.

My father-in-law was a very good cook and prepared pork belly and liver every day to build up Meitang's strength. My mother-in-law arrived from Linchuan, bringing hand-stitched shoes and hats for our baby. The house was full of cheerful bustle. The day Xizeng was one month old, we held a lively celebration in the noodle store.

On the business side, however, things were going poorly. Only the fresh noodles were selling, and not well. One night the shop was burgled, and the thief stole the medium-size noodle knife and went off with a bag of flour on his back too. We used the knife regularly, and once it was gone we could not make medium noodles anymore, only broad-cut and fine-cut ones. We first suspected the old noodle shop owner a hundred meters or so from our place of having put the culprit up to it, then we decided it must have been a Shandong man who sold herbal medicine and medicated patches nearby, because he was a big guy, proud of his martial arts skills. But there was nothing to prove it either way. Time passed, and the flour in the shop got too hot in the sunshine and became infested with weevils, which tainted the flavor. With that, business went from bad to worse.

2009.2.11.

One evening in July, a terrific commotion in the street outside caught my attention. I pushed open the window to see that the building opposite had caught fire and was blazing fiercely, blasting out a fearsome heat. Most ordinary homes in Nanchang were brick-and-timber constructions, the external walls of brick and the internal partitions of wood. When the weather was hot and dry, fires were an ever-present danger. Luckily for us, the wind was not blowing the flames toward our shop, and, although the windows were scorched by the heat, they did not catch fire. Meitang carried Xizeng back to the house at Chenjia Bridge, and Zhao Chunlin and I stayed to keep an eye on the shop. The fire raged until dawn, when it was finally extinguished.

By August, the shop had been open six months. According to Meitang's calculations, we were taking heavy losses. We looked at the figures and decided to close for good. We sold off the noodle cutter, counter, and our remaining stocks of flour at a knockdown price.

I looked everywhere for employment opportunities, but it was not easy. One day I spotted a flyer pasted to an electricity pole on the highway, advertising for recruits for a surveyors' team. I sent in my letter of application. I had some surveying training from my army days, and I could make maps, something I found very interesting. However, I received no response. I was probably considered untrustworthy because of my stint fighting with the Kuomintang Nationalist army.

On another occasion, I bumped into an old friend from my secondary school days, Pan Shangu. He worked at the Nanchang City Grain Bureau. He said they were short-staffed, the chief of the section trusted him, and he would be happy to introduce me. Not many days later, he told me his boss wanted to interview me. Their office, I saw when I arrived, was actually a classroom in a school. Where the teacher normally stood at the blackboard, a bench and two desks had been pushed together and did service as the office furniture. A man in his thirties, whom I took to be the section chief, sat at the desk. I introduced myself and sat down, and he asked me about my work history. But after I left, I heard nothing.

My father's sister in Nancheng had once employed a boy about my age, and when he finished his chores in the evenings, he would come and play with us (myself and my younger brother, and my nephews) in the back of the house. Later, he joined the People's Liberation Army and rose to be an officer. One day, he visited my father and my aunt in the house at Chenjia Bridge. I joined them, and we chatted about old times. He was looking well and talked about army life. When I returned to the shop afterward, I felt very depressed and went straight to bed in the little room behind the shop. Mei-tang saw the mood I was in and did her best to comfort me by talking about our future life together. I gradually cheered up and made up my mind that things would work out all right.

One day, when I was out looking for work, I saw a poster inviting people to apply for the Southeast Bookkeeping Training Courses. They were being run in the evenings in a school and taught bookkeeping, statistics, and shorthand. I felt that any kind of learning was a good thing and put my name down right away. We studied every evening from seven till nine for three months, and thus I acquired the rudiments of bookkeeping, although I was not sure what use I could put them to.

学初中同潘善毅，此时在粮
食局工作，他说该局正需
要招人，他能到科长去为
我介绍。某日，潘来告我，次

科长约我次日
去见面。

那时粮食局
连办公的地方都
没有，借用二间学
校教室用两班
课桌拼在一起，即
作为科长的办公
桌，其科长即
端坐在上方，对
面置一课凳（不
能说是椅凳，因无
靠背）便是我
的座位了。科长
询问也无非是
过去之经历而已，
我亦据实相告，
约半小时后辞
出。过了数日，消

息全无，连潘善毅
也看不到了……

某日我逛
街时，忽见
一广告，同东
离会计训练
班四招生培
训会计，统计，
速记人员。
为时半年，
每晚在某
校教室上课，
两小时，我即
报名参加学
习会计三个
月后即来去，
因我觉得统
计速记没有
什么用处。

Pan Shangu, a friend from my lower secondary school, was working in the Grain Bureau and told me they were recruiting. He offered to introduce me to the section chief, and one day came to tell me that his boss would see me the next day.

At that point, the Grain Bureau did not even have a proper office—they had taken over a school classroom, pushing together two desks for the chief to sit at. I perched on a stool opposite him (you could not call it a chair as it had no back). All he wanted to know about was what I had been doing up until then. I gave him the facts and about half an hour later was dismissed. Days passed and there was no news, and no sign of Pan Shangu either.

One day I was out for a stroll when I caught sight of an advertisement: the Southeast Bookkeeping Training Courses were enrolling students for bookkeeping, statistics, and shorthand courses lasting six months. Classes were run for two hours every evening. I signed up and attended for three months. I did not complete the course because I felt that statistics and shorthand were of no use to me.

Another day, I bumped into a friend from my third year in lower secondary school, Li Zhouguo. The other children used to call him Hand-to-Mouth, because his family was poor, but I never made fun of him and we got along well. On this occasion, he suggested, "Why don't we go into selling dried chilies together?" He had it all worked out: you could buy a large basket of chilies from the distributors for only two yuan and make a profit by selling them in small quantities. I had nothing better to do, so we partnered up and went to buy the chilies, carrying the basket away on a shoulder pole, one in front, one behind.

We arrived at a long street in a nearby suburb where there was a teahouse with seven or eight unpainted tables and benches. Street vendors were sitting around having a break and talking business, and there were four or five villagers too. They propped their baskets of vegetables and other produce on the stone steps at the door and sat down with their tea, ready to jump up and do a deal any time a passerby asked the prices. Otherwise, they sat there leisurely sipping tea, or smoking the occasional pipe.

We found a table. It was nine or ten o'clock in the morning on a bright, clear day, and the sunlight streaming into the teahouse was pleasantly warm. As we sipped our freshly brewed tea, I looked out at the passersby and thought that life was good.

The teahouse sold snacks too. We ordered some sweet rice-flour cake and a portion of "come-again," that is, refried breadsticks left over from the night before, and waited tranquilly for someone to favor us with their custom. No one did.

When it got to four o'clock in the afternoon, we picked up our basket of chilies on its shoulder pole and, one behind the other, headed back to the city. We repeated the operation the next day, sipping tea and eating snacks, but we had no customers and carried our wares home again. A week went by like this.

Then Li suggested we sell the chilies in the city. Obediently, I picked up my end of the shoulder pole, and we set off, one behind the other, with the basket of chilies between us. We had no vendor's license and could not go into the market, so we stopped outside the house of a wealthy family. About half an hour passed and a girl of eleven or twelve said she wanted to buy half a jin of chilies. This was our first piece of business. Li got out the balance scales, and I enthusiastically wrapped the chilies up in a piece of paper. I handed them over, and she paid. She had not been gone five minutes when a boy of about ten came rushing up and asked for half a jin. No business could be neglected, and we hastened to weigh the chilies out for him. Another four or five minutes passed and the first girl came running back and said she wanted another half jin.

The market

We were secretly delighted and began to feel that fortune was smiling on us. After we had done several transactions in quick succession, there was a pause, and Li sat down for a break. Suddenly he slapped his leg and cried: "A-ya! I've been an idiot!"

"What's up?" I asked, startled.

"I forgot about the pan!"

The balance scales was very rudimentary, and you had to take into account the weight of the brass pan every time you weighed the goods. Li had forgotten to do this, with the result that for every deal we did, we were effectively donating to our customers the equivalent weight in chilies. No wonder they came flocking.

Meitang and the family ribbed me mercilessly when I got home. "You'll never make a businessman! What trade have you been learning?" Thoroughly discouraged, Li and I decided to sell our chilies off cheap to the wholesalers we had bought them from and call it quits. And that was that.

Toward the end of the year, in mid-December, we received a letter from Thirteenth Uncle, a brother of my late mother's and manager of the Dade Hospital in Shanghai.[23] They needed an accountant. Would I take the job on?

Meitang, my father-in-law, and my father all thought this was an excellent idea and wanted me to set off without delay.

So I went to Nanchang station to buy a ticket. The place was deserted, with not a soul to be seen. I went into the booking hall through a small door. A tattered copy of the railway regulations was pasted on the wall, and on the right was a small round ticket window.

I bought the ticket and looked around again. All I could see was a pile of trash swept into one corner.

That night, my father and my aunt prepared a farewell dinner and invited my father-in-law too. After we had eaten, we sat there chatting and my father smoked his water pipe. Although we did not know it at the time, this was the last evening I was to spend with him.

In those days, I occasionally smacked Xizeng when he wailed especially loudly. That evening, Meitang complained about my behavior, and my father overheard: "You mustn't hit Xizeng ever again!" he exclaimed. "I'm going to mark out a no-hitting zone around him!" And he lit the twisted paper he used to light his pipe and drew circles in the air in front of our baby. Xizeng was only seven months old, and he stared, fascinated, his eyes following the lighted paper round and round.

It was the end of December and another early morning departure. I took a rickshaw to the station, my trunk placed under my feet. My father and aunt, Meitang, Third Brother and his wife, all stood at the door to see me off. The rickshaw puller picked up the handles, ready to set off. Something made me turn and take one last look at my father. Perhaps I sensed that I would never see him again.

I did not know it then, but the next time I would return to Nanchang city would be in 1958. So when we exchanged looks, it really was for the last time.

It was evening when I arrived in Shanghai. I hurriedly got a three-wheeler cab to Number 1136, Huashan Road, where Thirteenth Uncle and his wife awaited me on the doorstep. By then, it was night, and I went to sleep on an iron cot placed in my young cousin's room.

2009.3.4.

荫曾
丽珍
寿如
岳父
希曾
美棠
父亲
平如
姨姐

十月干脆我什么事也不干,在
家赋闲,晚上玩梭哈,时弟是
赢家,倒也快乐非凡。十二月
中旬,上海的十三舅忽来一信,
说大德医院总院需要一名
会计,希望我去上海担任此
职,闻此喜讯,父亲、岳父、美

左兰希曾脸前
转来转去,纸
烟在希曾眼
前绕绕,希曾
瞪大着眼睛,
骨碌碌地随着

着水烟,用纸捻(点火
用江西人称纸枚子)

梦多不宜多睡,捆过
几天就动身吧。众人
称是。此时父亲吸

灯下闲谈,惜惝着未来
的前景,父亲说着夜长

吃饭。饭后大家在厅堂
几个好菜,请岳父一道
用间姨姐备了

吸管
烟斗孔
烟斗筒
盖盒
烟草
水箱

左图:水烟筒署图
烟草又称黄烟,呈绒丝状置
入烟草盒内,用时取少许置烟
斗孔内,用纸捻吹着火后点燃烟
草,吸之,烟雾经过
水箱时发
呼噜之声。

李及全家人都非常开
心,是日晚间

那捻红的纸捻转个不停
……这是一个欢乐的夜晚。
因为,大家知道,从此我的便
有了一个稳定在社会上的
立脚之地,也便有了安定
的收入,平稳的生活,也从
而解除了父亲,岳父等人
对我们生活的担忧。

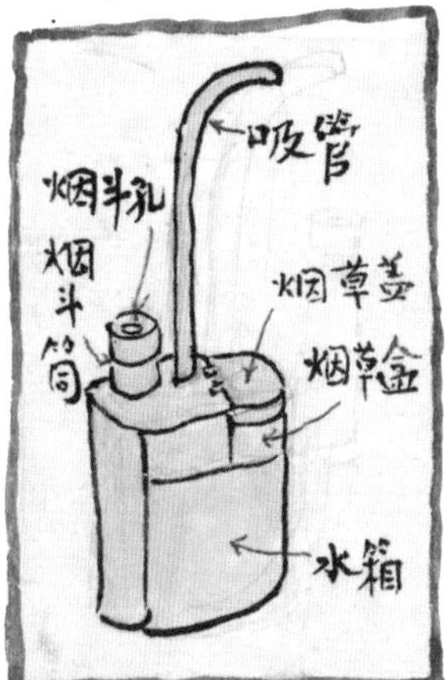

在车上我不禁回头再看了父亲一眼

ABOVE In the rickshaw, something made me turn and take one last look at my father.

OPPOSITE

TOP (left to right) Aunt, Pingru, Father, Xizeng, Meitang, Father-in-law, Shouru, Lizhen, Yinzeng

By October I had absolutely nothing to do and sat around twiddling my thumbs at home. My only amusement was playing poker in the evenings, which I thoroughly enjoyed and usually won. In mid-December, Thirteenth Uncle, a brother of my late mother's, wrote to say that the Dade Hospital in Shanghai needed an accountant. He wanted me to take the job on. The whole family—my father, father-in-law, Meitang, and everyone else—was delighted at this news. That evening, we had a splendid dinner, and my father-in-law joined us. After we had finished eating, we all gathered in the lamplit hall to talk excitedly about my future prospects. "Time and tide wait for no man, there's no point putting it off," said my father. "You should be on your way in a couple of days." There was general agreement. My father was smoking his water pipe and drew circles in the air with a lighted piece of twisted paper, leaving wisps of dark smoke hovering in front of Xizeng's face. Xizeng stared, fascinated, his eyes following the glowing red tip of the burning paper as it moved round and round. This was a happy evening. We were all aware that, with this job, I had obtained not only social status but also a steady income. Now that we were settled, my father and father-in-law no longer needed to worry about us.

OPPOSITE BOTTOM My father's water pipe

Clockwise from top: pipe stem, tobacco box lid, tobacco box, water box, tube, tube opening. The flossy shreds of pipe tobacco were kept in a small box. To smoke it, you took out a pinch, placed it in the tube, and lit it with the twisted paper. Once it was lit, you had to suck the pipe stem, so that the smoke passed through the water with a splurting sound, into the mouth, and out through the nostrils.

Meitang and I planned that I would take most of our belongings to Shanghai, and when I had found a place for us to live, she, Xizeng, her brother Aitang, and her sister Youtang would follow. At first, we rented a place in Shoukang Alley, off Shandong South Road. Later, I found a two-room apartment at Number 18, Xin Yong An Road, for which I paid seven ounces of gold. As the years went by here, children were born and grew up, traveled away, came home, and left again; and here under this roof Meitang and I lived for more than half a century.

上海市黄浦区新永安路18号门前之示意图

我们初来上海时住在山东南路寿康里8号（一间，10平才来）一九五二年夏迁至此处（两间，36平六来），直到二〇〇三年六月近至闵行区航新路，我们全家在这里生活了半个多世纪—五十一年。

Sketch of the entrance of Number 18, Xin Yong An Road, Huangpu district, Shanghai

Our first home in Shanghai, a one-room apartment of ten square meters. In the summer of 1952, we moved to Xin Yong An Road, where we had two rooms, thirty-six square meters. The whole family stayed here for a total of fifty-one years, until June 2003, when we moved to Hangxin Road, in the Minhang district of Shanghai.

大德医院院长
大德出版社社长
杨元吉（我的舅公）

大德医院医务主任
大德医院分院院长
章玉玲（我的舅母）

大德医院的办公室

The office at Dade Hospital

Left to right: Head of Dade Hospital/Director of Dade Publications, Yang Yuanji (Thirteenth Uncle); my aunt Zhang Yuling (Thirteenth Uncle's wife); Accountant/Arts and Literature Editor, Pingru; Director of Medicine/Head of Dade Hospital (Branch Hospital)

When I started, I was doing two jobs at Dade Hospital, and earning two salaries. One was as the hospital accountant, using my newly acquired knowledge. The other was as editor at Dade Publications, which was where my chief interests lay. In those days, our life as a family together in Shanghai went on busily and cheerfully.

At the beginning of the fifties, Shanghai was a lively, bustling place to live. Every weekend the trade unions in many workplaces organized "friendship dances," and Dade Hospital was no exception. Meitang loved to dance and meet her friends, and she never missed an occasion. Back then, privately run dance halls were still open, and Meitang and I often went to them to enjoy ourselves as well.

OPPOSITE

TOP LEFT **Wife sings, husband accompanies her**
TOP RIGHT "Clouds disperse, the bright moon shines down, and we two are filled with happiness.
On the pond's bright waters, a devoted pair of mandarin ducks play.
Red blooms and green leaves, twin lotus flowers on one stalk.
Everything loving comes in pairs.
The warm breeze wafts over beautiful flowers.
Sweet tenderness is all around."
—Lyrics from "Flowers in Bloom, a Full Moon"

浮雲散明月照人未困圆美
滿今朝最。清淺池塘鴛鴦
戲水。紅裳翠蓋並蒂蓮
開。雙雙對之恩恩愛愛。
這暖風兒正對着好花兒吹。
柔情蜜意滿人間。

壬辰四月平如學畫，時年九十

妇唱夫随

Finally, I was in step with Meitang.

TOP "It's too far away, I can't see!"

BOTTOM "This seat's fine, I can see perfectly." "Oh! Right! I can see too clearly!"

半斤八两

Two of a kind

LEFT "Excuse me, Auntie, which is the hearted cabbage?" RIGHT "You've planted so many garlic chives, however will you eat them all?"

When we weren't dancing, we went to films. I had perfect vision, but Meitang was nearsighted. If we sat in the middle or back rows, she couldn't see the screen properly. So we sat in the front rows. As time went on, I became nearsighted too. Finally, I was in step with Meitang.

During the War Against Japan, Meitang and her parents had taken refuge from the bombing in a village near Hankou. When she first saw paddy rice seedlings, she thought they were garlic chives and became the laughingstock of the village.

For my part, I had never been to a market until we went food shopping in Shanghai, and the fact that I couldn't tell a hearted cabbage from Chinese leaves made me the laughingstock this time. These stories became the stuff of family jokes for many years.

痛不痛？

哎哟！

向美棠宣传"无痛分娩法"

Promoting "pain-free childbirth" to Meitang

LEFT "Does it hurt?" RIGHT "A-ya!"

I was the editor for *Mother and Child Health,* one of Dade Publications' magazines, where I once read an article by Pavlov about "pain-free childbirth." I hurried home with this gem of wisdom and told Meitang all about it. Meitang listened to what I had to say, then said skeptically, "Is this Pavlov a man or a woman?" "A man . . ." Before I had finished speaking, Meitang pinched my thigh viciously. "Does it hurt?" she asked calmly.

"Yes! Yes!" I yelled.

"When women give birth, how would you men know whether it hurts or not?" she said.

美棠用指甲划肤断案

Meitang delivering a verdict after running her fingernails along Guobin's arm

"You've been swimming again in the Huangpu, haven't you?"

Meitang dealt systematically with any mischief from the children. In those days, the Huangpu River filled with children swimming in summer. Our second son, Guobin, adored swimming, and when he was twelve, he swam right across the Huangpu.[24]

But he was still a little boy, and for reasons of safety, the River Police sent regular patrols to stop young children from swimming. When the children saw them coming, they would scatter in all directions and hide. Guobin once hid under a boat, which was extremely dangerous. After that, Meitang expressly forbade him from swimming. But Guobin found a way: when he returned to shore, he lay on the bank and got nice and dry before going home, convinced that his mother would never catch him. Meitang's response was to grab his arm and run her fingernail along it: it left the kind of white mark that skin has when it has been immersed in water. "You've been swimming again!" she exclaimed.

顺曾走丢了

Maotou gets lost.

Text on red banner: "Serve the People"

There were a lot of street parades in those days, and our youngest son, Maotou, loved to see them go by. Once, when he was four, he followed them and got lost. We looked everywhere, but no one had seen him. We were frantic. Meitang suggested we should make inquiries with every local police station, and, sure enough, on my way to Songshan Road station, I was told that some people had taken a lost child there. I rushed over on my bicycle. By that time it was dark. I arrived to see Maotou sitting on a Ping-Pong table eating a bun the policeman had given him while someone else played the flute to amuse him. He was having a lovely time!

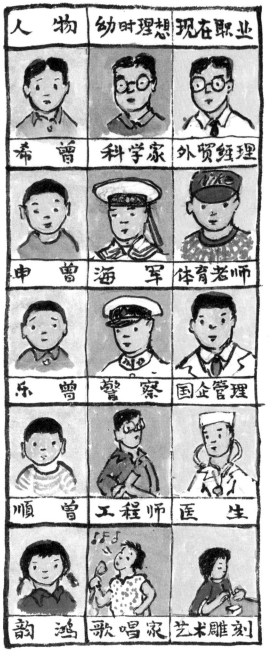

孩子们在小时候曾画下自己的理想，但现实生活改变了一切。把现在的职业与过去的理想列表加以对照，从而看到了他们的人生轨迹。

When they were small, the children made drawings of what they wanted to be when they grew up. But real life changed all that. If we compare their dreams with their jobs now, we can see where their lives actually took them.

CHILD	CHILDHOOD AMBITION	OCCUPATION TODAY
Xizeng	Scientist	Foreign trade director
Shenzeng (Guobin)	The navy	P.E. teacher
Lezeng	Policeman	State enterprise manager
Shunzeng (Maotou)	Engineer	Doctor
Yunhong	Singer	Arts engraver

"Family Pictures"

I gave the children a picture album, with "Family Pictures" in large writing on the front, and encouraged them all to paint pictures of their thoughts and what they saw around them. Looking at one another's efforts made it even more interesting.

When they were small, they all drew pictures of their ambitions. But real life changed all that.

Beginning in 1957, there was a drastic change in the political climate. On September 28, 1958, I was taken to Anhui province to do Reeducation Through Labor. Thus began a separation from my family that lasted twenty-two years.

They quickly became almost destitute. It was during those years of turmoil that the five children were passing through the most important period of their youth, growing to adulthood, studying and learning skills, being sent to labor in the countryside, working, and falling in love. My mother-in-law grew older, and the whole family I had left behind languished in poverty. The arduous task of holding it all together fell to Meitang. She and I saw so many families being wrenched apart by quarrels and by destitution. Fortunately, it never entered our heads to split up.

When winter is at its coldest,
spring cannot be far behind.

6
You Ask Me When I Will Return

Not many days after I was sent to do Reeducation Through Labor, Personnel at my work sent someone to talk to Meitang. They advised her to divorce me (as they put it in those days, "make a clean break" between us). Meitang took no notice.

Many years later, Meitang and I were talking about this, and she said: "If you'd had an affair, I would have divorced you immediately . . . but you hadn't betrayed your country, you hadn't embezzled anything, you hadn't been a thief, you hadn't done anything wrong, why would I divorce you?"

In 1958, our eldest son, Xizeng, was only nine years old, but he understood that difficult times lay ahead.[25] The campaign to smelt iron and steel was in full swing, and one day he was walking along the Shanghai Bund when he saw a group of workers banging away at a pile of scrap iron and moving it across the road. Xizeng stopped to watch, and someone asked him: "You want to come and help?" He nodded. So the workers gave him a small piece to carry. He did this all morning, and at the end of it, they gave him fifty cents. Xizeng went home and gave the money to his mother. When Meitang found out what had happened, she was horrified and begged him never to do anything like that again.

划清界线

"Make a clean break!"

希曾9岁时在外滩搬运钢铁

Nine-year-old Xizeng carrying scrap iron across the Bund

在上海自然博物館工地上背水泥

Meitang carrying bags of cement at the Natural History Museum construction site

In order to boost the family income, Meitang took any extra work that came her way. She even carried bags of cement on the construction site of the Natural History Museum nearby. A bag of cement weighed at least fifty jin, and the work caused long-term damage to her back and kidneys.

We were separated by distance, but we never stopped writing to each other. When the children were bigger, they kept in touch by letter too.

还差一分钱

One cent short!

Near the Liu An Gear Factory, where I had been sent, was a kiosk that sold postage stamps. One evening after dinner, I happened to have finished a letter and went to post it. I could feel some small change in my pocket, but I couldn't be bothered to count it. I went up to the counter and asked the woman for an eight-cent stamp. Then I counted out the money: one cent, two cents, three cents, four cents, five cents, six cents, seven cents . . . and that was all! I was one cent short. The shop assistant took the stamp back and I had to pick up my money and leave with the letter unposted.

神奇的乳白鱼肝油

Miraculous cod-liver oil

In the autumn of 1959, right in the middle of the Three Years of Natural Disasters, I suddenly developed edema. My abdomen swelled up like a balloon, as if the skin had separated from the flesh, while my legs shrank to sticks, no more than twenty centimeters in diameter. There was no pain or itching, it was just difficult to walk. The infirmary at work gave me sick leave, but there was no medication available. As luck would have it, that very day I received a parcel from Meitang containing a bottle of cod-liver oil.

美棠因腰痛去看病

Meitang saw a doctor about her back pain.

So that morning, when the usual bucket of red beans and rice appeared and I had filled my enamel mug, I poured almost half the bottle of oil onto the steaming rice and mixed it in. It suddenly seemed to me as if these rice and beans were the most delicious thing in the world. I felt so good when I'd eaten them. I finished every drop of the oil that day and the next, and the edema gradually subsided until I was back to normal.

Meitang went to the hospital about her chronic back pain. The doctor gave her a prescription, but it was going to cost two yuan (sixty cents). Meitang did the math and figured that the medication would come to more than twelve yuan a month. Where would she get this kind of money? She never went back to the doctor.

大家來看看他的"八卦衣"!

Everyone came to look at his Eight Trigrams robe!

Meitang's mother was exceptionally good at needlework and was constantly mending and sprucing up the children's threadbare clothing, collecting pieces of fabric of all colors to use as patches, then dyeing them all indigo blue. The results looked like new. Once Lezeng went to school wearing one of these garments, so patched it looked like a Peking Opera character's Eight Trigrams robe. His teacher gasped in admiration. She took him to the office just to show the other teachers his grandmother's exquisite "handicraft work."

我的"小发明"之一
——铅丝、车胎补鞋法

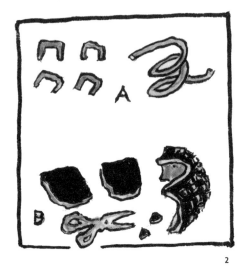

One of my "inventions": mending shoes with wire and a rubber tire

1. Worn-out shoes, with a hole in each heel. 2. (A) First, take a length of stout wire and make four staples about two centimeters wide, with a pair of pliers. (B) Then take an old pushcart tire and cut two squares of rubber roughly the size of the heels. 3. Punch holes in each heel and insert the staples, attaching the rubber pieces. Then hammer the staples flat, and the job is done. In my experience, this method could extend the life of shoes for between four and six months.

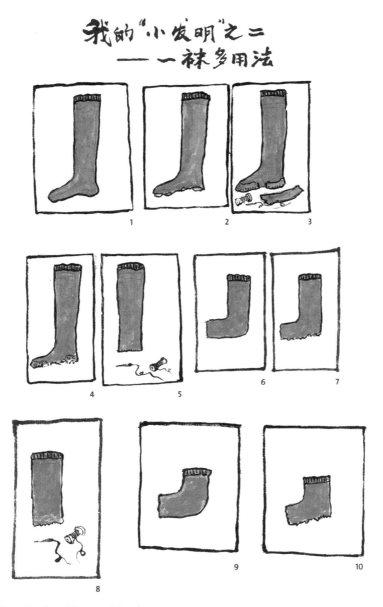

我的"小发明"之二
——一袜多用法

My second "invention": making a sock last longer

1. Long socks. 2. Holes develop in the sole and heel. 3. Patch them with a thick piece of cloth. 4. The mended socks develop new holes. 5. Cut off the worn parts and sew them up. 6. They are now midlength socks. 7. The midlength socks develop holes. 8. Cut off the worn parts and sew them up. 9. They are now short socks. 10. The short socks develop holes and can be thrown away.

伴我十年的列宁装

1

2

3

4

The "Lenin jacket" that lasted me ten years

1. At the beginning of the fifties, Lenin jackets were the height of fashion. I bought one and kept it for best, wearing it for Chinese New Year and other holidays, or important meetings and conferences. In the autumn of 1958, after I was sent to Anhui, Meitang unstitched and removed its fur collar and mailed me the jacket, so that I had something to keep me warm. 2. Five years later. 3. Ten years later. I had made various additions to the jacket, sewing on layers of patches, and finally covering it in a white sheet sewn together firmly with strong thread. I had no buttons, so when I wore it, I tied it around the waist. This garment had three main uses: it kept the wind and cold out (its primary use); it kept the rain out, because it was so thick; and I used it as a pillow when I slept. It immediately warmed me under the quilt—after several years of patching, it weighed more than ten jin. 4. In the summer of 1968, I was transferred to the Liu An Gear Factory and left the Huai River containment project, where I had done ten years of Reeducation Through Labor. By this point, my jacket was in retirement. I folded it neatly and left it in the shed where I used to sleep. Before I left, I took a long look at it. Through all those severe winters, that jacket had kept me reliably warm.

When the children were happy

The family was issued "cake and biscuit vouchers" every month. Meitang would use them to buy taitiao (a kind of seaweed) and fried dough twists for the children, their favorite treat. She distributed the dough twists, one per child, in the evening after dinner when they were doing their homework.

六分钱菜票度过三天之行动计划

	早	中	晚
第一天	盐		
第二天	盐		
第三天	盐		
方法	1.早上买2分钱的咸菜一碟，但不吃，以盐代之。 2.中午吃半碟咸菜。 3.晚上吃半碟咸菜。		

Without the aid of Meitang's clever planning, I would have been in dire straits.

Three-day action plan for six cents' worth of food coupons: 1. In the morning, I bought a saucer of pickled cabbage for 2 cents, but I did not eat it, just made do with the salt. 2. At midday, I ate half the saucer of pickled cabbage. 3. And at the evening meal, I ate the other half.

At the beginning of 1960, Meitang started work in a community workshop in the Huangpu district.[26] She was extremely competent, and it fell to her to make notes and keep records. Sometimes, there was a new component to be assembled, and it was always Meitang who went to the factory and learned how to do it, then returned to teach her fellow workers.

They had to work in pairs, and everyone wanted to work with Meitang because that way they would produce plenty of good-quality pieces without having to exert themselves too much. The community workshop leader had great confidence in Meitang, and if there were any problems or disputes on the team, she always came to discuss them with her. Meitang was friendly and resourceful, and the other women regularly asked her to write documents or family letters for them. Meitang hurried home at midday every day to tidy up and fix a meal for the children. If she had time, she wrote to me, or wrote letters for her fellow workers. And then there was the queuing, which took up a lot of time.

美棠替生产组的同事写信

Meitang wrote letters for her fellow workers in the community workshop.

生产组小组长来我家找美棠商量事情

The workshop leader came to our house to discuss matters with Meitang.

Lunchtime entertainment: eating "pistols"

1. When Meitang was working in the community workshop, she hurried home at midday every day to fix a meal for the children. 2. But sometimes, if there was no time, she got them to do it themselves. She gave each of the children a small lump of dough, so they could make their own pancakes. 3. Maotou, our fourth son, always had creative ideas for games. When it was his turn to make his pancake, he shaped it into a pistol and made a "pistol pancake." 4. "Don't move!" he commanded them, pointing the "pistol" at his older brothers' heads. 5. Our second son, Guobin, bit off half the pistol barrel in one bite. 6. The gunman's attempt at bravado fell flat when he lost half his lunch. He burst into floods of tears!

变脸

From smile to glare

The whole family was stigmatized because I was doing Reeducation Through Labor. Meitang, in Shanghai, suffered more than just material hardship. She told me that she remembered once going to see "Auntie Fan," the cadre in charge of their alley.[27] The woman had her back to her, so Meitang called out: "Auntie Fan!" The instant the woman turned around and caught sight of Meitang, her beaming smile froze on her face. How fickle our fellow humans are!

無处求助 祷告苍天

Meitang praying to the heavens, her last resort

In 1968, our eldest, Xizeng, graduated from middle school. Meitang was desperately eager for him to get a job in a state-owned industry. That way he could contribute to the family income and help around the house too. But the Propaganda Team who allocated work to the new graduates insisted on sending him to the countryside. If he was working on a rural commune, not only would he not be able to help but he would continue to need financial support. Meitang begged them again and again to reconsider, but to no avail. One night, our daughter, Yunhong, woke up to see her mother kneeling on the balcony praying to the heavens. There really was no one else she could turn to.

给熟睡中的女儿戴上金手镯

She put the bracelet on the wrist of her sleeping daughter.

Two days later, the Propaganda Team was transferred elsewhere and a new team arrived. As soon as Guobin heard the news, he told his mother, who rushed to the school and explained their situation once more. The new team head agreed to Meitang's request and gave Xizeng a job in the Shanghai Radio Factory. Maybe heaven really had taken pity on her.

As the years went by, Meitang gradually sold off the family's belongings. The children used to sit out on the street from a very young age, selling her beads by the handful. Meitang had received five pairs of gold bracelets as a dowry, but finally there was only one left. The night before she was going to sell that last bracelet, she looked sadly

当掉了羊皮袄子

She pawned the lambskin robe.

at little Yunhong, who was fast asleep in bed. Parents always want to leave their children something nice, but from now on she would have nothing left to leave. She put the bracelet on her daughter's wrist and left it on all night. When the next day came, she took it off and went out to sell it.

In 1969, Guobin and Lezeng were sent to work on a commune in the Jiangsu countryside. By this time, Meitang had sold almost everything she had. The only thing of value she had left was the lambskin robe, the single gift she had chosen from the things my late mother left to her daughters-in-law. Meitang was very fond of it and always hoped she would have it to keep her warm when she got old. But the two children working on communes needed to be supplied with daily necessities. It would have to go to the pawnshop. She hurried all the way from New North Gate to Old West Gate, chose the priciest pawnshop, and got sixty yuan for it. These were drastic measures for the direst of times. Her pawn tickets piled up in the metal bowl, but there was no way she could redeem her possessions.

一张"可怜"的小木桌

A "poor little" wooden table

Shop sign reads: "We Take Secondhand Goods."

At some point in the 1950s, I had bought a small lightweight table, at which the family ate their meals, Meitang did her sewing, and the children their homework.

Nearly twenty years sped by, and the children were all grown up. The table was ready for retirement, but they kept it usable with a nail here or a piece of wire there, though it was unsteady on its feet and the paint was flaking off.

In Guobin's commune, labor and timber were cheap, so he had a set of furniture made and sent it to Shanghai. It included an Eight Immortals table, so called because it was square and seated eight. There was nowhere to put the old table, and Meitang told Lezeng to try to get a bit of cash for it. Lezeng took it to the secondhand store and asked for two yuan. He handed it over to the storekeeper, who chucked it into a corner. The table landed on the floor and lay there, the frame askew. Lezeng, a sensitive child, felt so sorry for it that he cried.

为了不让脑子过于"清闲"，我一边
劳动，一边读书。

I studied in order to keep my brain working.

During my first ten years in Anhui, I was assigned to a Huai River containment project. The labor was unskilled and primitive, and did not occupy my mind at all. In order to keep my brain working, I copied some sentences from an English textbook Meitang had sent me onto scraps of paper. During the winter, I kept these scraps in my jacket pocket, and in summer, in my straw hat. When we took a break from our labors, I would take them out and recite them. At least this provided a pleasant distraction from the relentless toil.

蚊帳裡面練指法

"Practicing" under the mosquito net

Later on, I borrowed a violin from my brother-in-law for a while and started to learn to play it. But the noise disturbed people I shared the dormitory with, so I made myself a rectangular piece of wood and marked on it the positions of the strings and the frets. Then, in the evening, I got under my mosquito net and "practiced" on this pretend violin. On Sunday, a rest day, I could leave the work site and find somewhere to practice on the real thing.

快到家了，我挑着重担 快步前进

Almost home, I hurried along, carrying the heavy bags on a shoulder pole.

The Chinese New Year was always the high point of the year. This was the one time I could visit home. These trips back were my most exciting and busiest time, and I started making preparations a good two weeks beforehand. First, I arranged holiday leave, then I borrowed money, around three hundred yuan, to spend on things to take to the family. Some things were hard to find or very expensive in Shanghai, so I had endless discussions with Meitang about what to get: glutinous rice, peanuts, sesame seeds, soybeans, melon seeds, vegetable oil, sesame oil, eggs, salted duck, and so on.

The day of my departure, I would set off at the crack of dawn, carrying my bags on a shoulder pole to Liu An bus station, five or six li distant. The bus took me to Hefei city, where I boarded a train. From Shanghai station, I put on a final spurt for the two-hour walk along Henan Road, to my home.

快要过年喽！多么开心呀！……
The New Year will soon be here. How happy we are!

Lyrics (left to right): "Plunging through immense forests, striding undaunted over snowy plains!"[28] "Graceful birch standing tall, remote blue skies.... Ah, spring is coming to the country of the north!"[29]

The whole family was thrilled to see me. It was always evening by the time I arrived, and my mother-in-law would be at the stove on the walkway where we did our cooking, steaming a salted duck. Meitang and Yunhong would be frying melon seeds and peanuts over a coal briquette stove indoors, filling the room with a delicious smell. The children sang at the top of their voices, and I got out my harmonica and accompanied them. Our neighbor, old Mrs. Wu, would sigh as she passed our door: "Such a lovely family!" The two weeks of the Spring Festival holiday passed all too quickly.

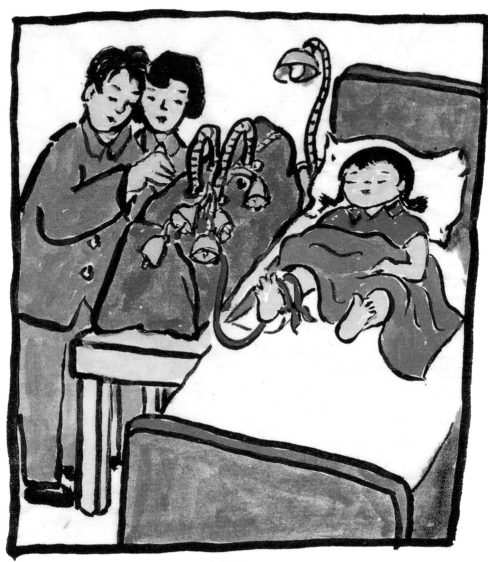

小红脚上的绳子和铃铛

The rope and bells attached to Yunhong's foot

One year I had bought my train ticket back and was due to leave the next morning. Only Xizeng and Guobin were allowed to accompany me to the station. The little ones wanted to come too, but I would not let them. After some argument, our youngest, Yunhong, suddenly smiled. "I know what to do!" she said.

When it got light, I prepared to go. I went to fetch the big travel bag. It seemed to be stuck on something. When I looked closely, I could see bells tied to the bag, and those bells were also tied with a string to Yunhong's right foot. I carefully undid the string without waking my sleeping daughter. Glancing again at her, I picked up the bag and left with Xizeng and Guobin. Meitang said goodbye to me at the door. I did not allow her to come any farther either.

At the beginning of 1979, rumors began to circulate at the factory to the effect that people who were originally registered with a Shanghai *hukou* could transfer back there, providing their families were willing to receive them. But there were risks. By that time, we had steady jobs at the factory, which brought health insurance, pensions, and other benefits. The wages I sent home every month were the mainstay of the family. If I returned to Shanghai and could not get a job, I would be plunging the family into even worse poverty.

返回上海后第一张全家福照片

The first photograph of the whole family after my return to Shanghai

I discussed the options over and over with Meitang and our children, and finally decided to come home. And so, in November 1979, I officially gave my notice at the gear factory and signed an agreement that I would never go back there or make any demands of them again. Meitang and the children had been making preparations for my return for months, gathering information, and writing letters to the authorities asking that my case, and the accusations against me, be reexamined.

Finally, on November 16, I arrived back in Shanghai. The next day, I went to register for my *hukou*. A week later, we all went to a photography studio to have a family picture taken. Guobin was still laboring on the commune and was not able to get back, so his image was added in later.

It took the Shanghai municipal police until December 19, 1980, to make their decision: they quashed my sentence to Reeducation Through Labor and restored my salary and position in my original workplace. When winter is at its coldest, spring cannot be far behind.

Her desires were simple but they were destined never to be fulfilled.
"Other lives we cannot divine, this life is finished." And lamenting over it is fruitless!

7

Now You Are Gone

I returned to work at my old publishing house. The children now had jobs and were settled: Xizeng was still at the Radio Factory, Guobin was in Jiangsu, teaching in a middle school, but Lezeng had "responded to the government's call" and come back to Shanghai. Maotou was in his second year at the hospital, and Yunhong was about to get married and move out.

In time, grandchildren began to arrive. We were still poor, but life felt good. Every evening, I sat at my desk reading manuscripts, and Meitang lay on the bed, teaching songs to our granddaughter Shushu. I remembered similarly good, tranquil times on visits to my maternal grandmother's house when we were children. I remembered the red paper strip pasted across the lintel of my granny's bedroom door. It read: "Happiness, long life, good health, and peace." In old age, that's all people want, and have always wanted.

On the morning of June 20, 1982, I suffered sharp pains in the chest and abdomen, and Meitang rushed me to Ruijin Hospital. The next day I was diagnosed with acute pancreatitis and was operated on immediately. When the doctor explained what was wrong with me, Meitang was horrified. Her hands shook so much that she was unable to sign the consent form and one of the children had to sign instead. The operation was a great success, but I was not allowed to eat or drink for seventeen days and had to be tube-fed. On Day 18, I felt the urge to open my bowels, but my stools had become impacted because I was confined to bed. Meitang had to dig the feces out with her finger, and then I was able to defecate normally.

在安宁中感受幸福

Enjoying a peaceful life

Meitang sings to Shushu: "Little swallow in a black and white jacket …"

夏天的早晨

A summer morning

Meitang and I used to buy our vegetables, then sit together shucking fresh soybeans.

在医院的走廊上等待着

Waiting on the hospital walkway

I spent a month in the hospital recuperating. Meitang got up at five every morning to queue up for snakehead fish, which she made into soup for me. Then she hastened to Ruijin Hospital (visiting hours began at three o'clock in the afternoon) with her food container, riding the Number 12 bus to Ruijin Number Two Road. She walked the short distance to the rear entrance of the hospital and arrived each day at about a quarter past three. The ward was on the second floor, and as the time for her arrival drew near, I would go out onto the walkway to keep a lookout. I could just see her, lunch box in hand, as she passed down a narrow alley, and that was my cue to hurry back to bed. A few minutes later, she would come in, puffing and panting, quickly open the lunch box, and urge me to eat while the soup was still warm.

Those few minutes every afternoon are still vivid in my memory. Sadly, the patient who waited for his daily soup is still hale and hearty, but the bringer of the soup has left him forever.

看海豚，我成了落汤鸡

Drowned rats after the dolphin show

Once, when our grandson Yuanyuan was eight years old, the Huangpu Sports Center held a dolphin show. I felt this was not to be missed and took Yuanyuan to see it. On the way back, we got caught in heavy rain. I did not have an umbrella with me, so I gave Yuanyuan a piggyback ride, and we hurried home, hopping from the shelter of one overhanging roof to the next. What fun grandparents can have with the little ones! Braving the rain that day with my grandson on my back seemed like a great game. I was then sixty-six, and Meitang was sixty-three.

乐曾巧做"麦淀粉水饺"

Lezeng was adept at making wheat starch dumplings.

Meitang was suffering from kidney problems and was finally diagnosed with diabetes. The ideal food for diabetics is wheat starch, because it is low in protein and fat. But it is also difficult to cook, because it does not stick together like wheat flour. Lezeng knew a lot about food preparation, and he was very patient. He mixed the wheat starch with hot water and carefully experimented with the proportions until he succeeded in producing a dough which he could roll out into dumpling skins. We stuffed them with minced vegetables and boiled or steamed them. Meitang enjoyed them very much.

耳听是虚，眼见为实

Seeing is believing.

Meitang scolded me for being useless at everything!

"The food is overcooked!" "And too salty!" "You've left the drawer open!" "You spilled water on the floor when you were washing your face!" "You can't even buy the right book! Shushu wanted a language textbook in the New Concept series, and you bought her a book called *New Concepts*!"

In 2004 I was admitted to Zhongshan Hospital with angina and had a coronary bypass. The operation was a great success. I spent a week there recuperating, and the children took turns to keep me company. Meitang was not in good health, so they would not let her make the trip on the day of the operation, reassuring her that all had gone well. But she was still worried and persuaded her granddaughter Shushu to take her to visit me the day after. When she saw I was doing well, she finally relaxed. She spent some time chatting with me and went home in good spirits.

Our cat, however, refused to move or eat for three or four days because I was not there. That was another source of anxiety for Meitang: "Pussy is terribly depressed!" she told Shushu. "You must play with her, and give her shredded pork to eat!" When I was finally discharged and got back home, it was not only Meitang who was delighted; the cat leaped in the air, meowing loudly as she wove in and out around my legs.

Siesta

Finally, I had a faithful listener.

A hard question to answer

"Why didn't you learn to paint when you were a kid? You'd be a painter by now if you had! What's the point of starting now?"

Once I had retired, I had time on my hands and began in earnest to learn painting: I got myself paints, xuanzhi art paper, and Chinese painting instruction books, and started work. Every time I finished a painting, I showed it to Meitang, but most of the time, she laughed at my efforts. When I had started at Nanchang Number One Middle School as a boy, I heard that the famous painter Mr. Fu Baoshi used to be the art teacher, but sadly he had left before I arrived. I joked with Meitang that under his guidance I would have painted much better than I did now. She used to make fun of me when I said that, but mostly she scolded me for not having started earlier.

Our children were doing quite well for themselves by now, and one spring day we arranged to go to Nanxiang for a meal of steamed xiaolong dumplings. By then, Meitang needed a wheelchair to go out, but she was in very good spirits. We found a restaurant that was clean and smart, and Meitang ate with a good appetite. After we had eaten, we took her for a stroll around Guyi Park. After that, right up until she became very sick and confused, she talked often about going back to Nanxiang for a meal of steamed dumplings.

到南翔去吃小笼

Eating xiaolong dumplings in Nanxiang

Meitang's kidneys were failing, and she needed daily peritoneal dialysis. I went to the hospital to consult the nursing staff, bought the necessary equipment, and performed the dialysis on her at home. We did that for four years.

Illustration of home dialysis

LABELS CLOCKWISE FROM 12:00 Dialysate in its bag, infusion tube, pull ring, drainage tube, waste bucket, empty bag (drainage bag), infusion and drainage tubes, iodine cap, connector, abdominal catheter, antiseptic wipes.

TOP RIGHT Warm cabinet. BOTTOM RIGHT Scales.

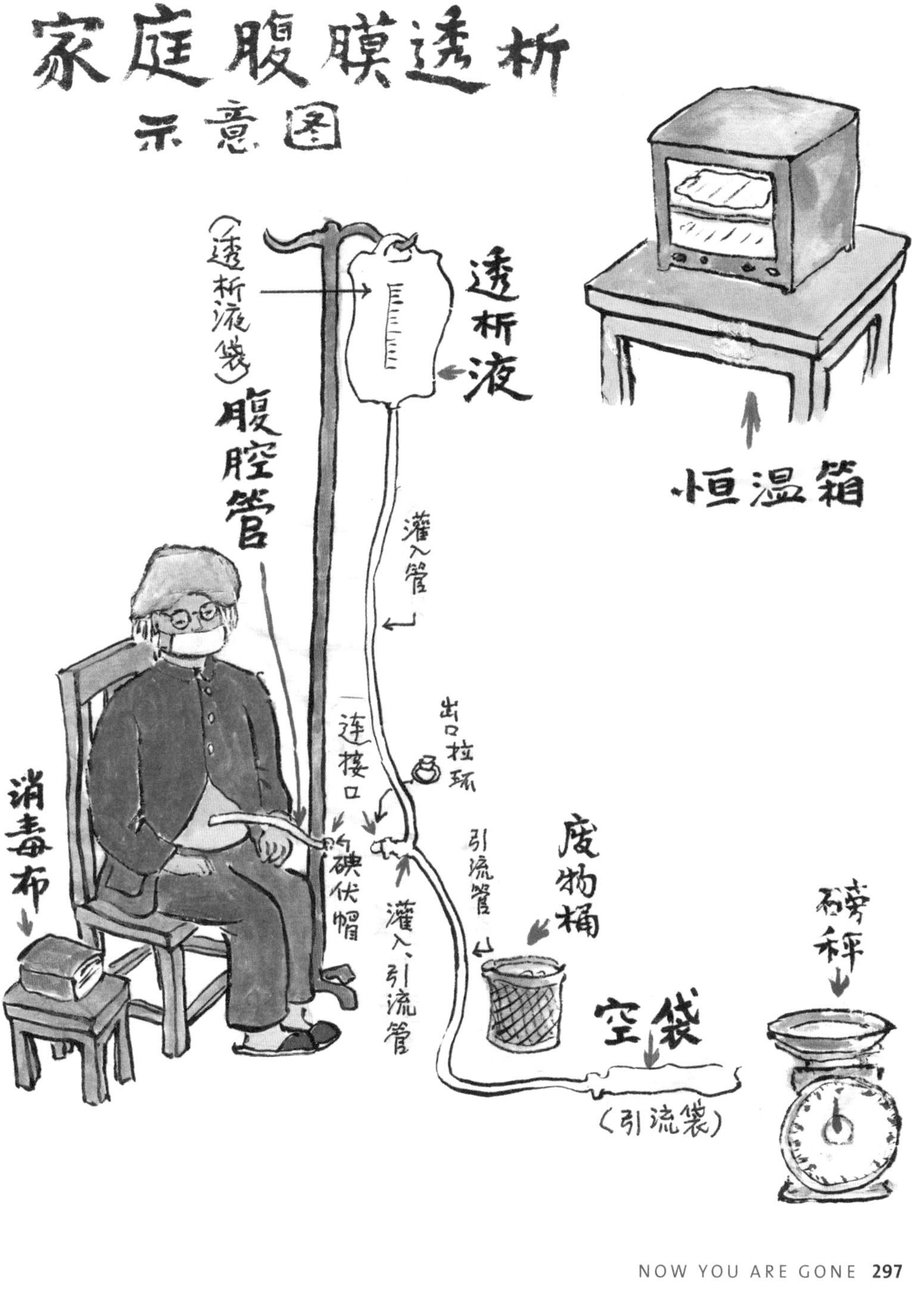

家庭腹膜透析
示意图

透析液袋
透析液
腹腔管
灌入管
恒温箱
连接口
出口拉环
碘伏帽
引流管
废物桶
消毒布
灌入、引流管
空袋
（引流袋）
磅秤

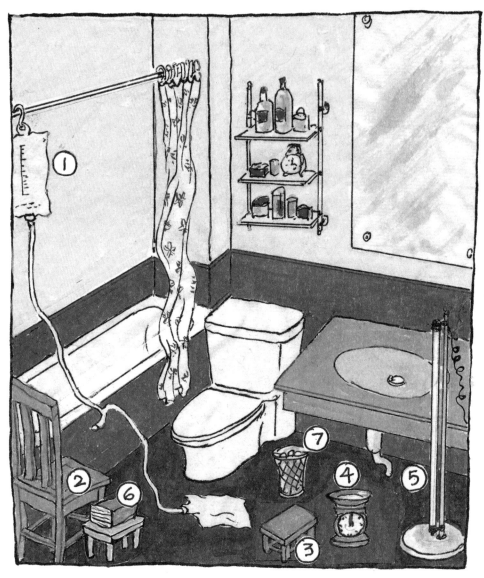

我家的"腹膜透析室"

Our dialysis room at home

1. Dialysate bag. 2. Meitang's wooden chair. 3. My stool. 4. Scales. 5. Ultraviolet strip light. 6. Antiseptic wipes.
7. Wastebasket.

I chose our en-suite bathroom as the dialysis room, because it was easy to keep clean. This was the procedure:

First, the whole room, including the ceiling, was cleaned. Then formalin disinfectant was sprayed everywhere. Finally, the ultraviolet light was left on for thirty minutes. We had to ensure a sterile environment. The ultraviolet light was designed by my son-in-law: he found a heavy metal disk in a flea market to serve as the base, and fixed a vertical metal rod into it. Then he bought an ultraviolet light tube and attached it to the rod. The whole contraption was compact and easy to move.

I asked the hospital nurse to instruct me in what to do. I got her to take me through the whole procedure, step by step, and I made diagrams as she demonstrated. Then I went home and wrote all my notes up in the form of a table, which I stuck to the wall behind Meitang's chair. I read each step, then performed it. I could not afford to be careless.

Before doing the dialysis, both Meitang and I put on cotton masks and washed our hands with disinfectant soap.

The dialysate bag hung from the shower curtain rail.

Meitang sat on the chair. The infusion stage took about forty minutes, while the drainage took less than half an hour. To make Meitang more comfortable, I bought a folding chair with back support and seat cushions, and a canvas-covered and a bamboo recliner chair, but none of them were ideal. They were either too hard or too low, so that the tube did not drain properly. In the end, we went back to the wooden chair.

After the catheter and infusion/drainage tube had been connected, the connector was covered with an antiseptic wipe to keep it sterile and placed on Meitang's knee.

When I had finished setting things up, I could sit on my stool and take a rest. The iodine cap and the pull ring were then discarded into the wastebasket.

1. Hold the catheter in the left hand between ring and little fingers, and hold the infusion/drainage tube in the right hand between ring and little fingers. Hold the tip of each tube about 2 centimeters apart.

2. Rotate both wrists inward to bring the catheter and the tube close.

3. Pull the pull ring off the end of the tube held in the right hand, with the thumb and index finger of the left hand, and immediately discard it into the wastebasket. (This exposes the threaded connector to the air.)

4. With the thumb and forefinger of the right hand, rotate the iodine cap on the tip of the catheter inward to unscrew, remove, and immediately discard it. (This exposes the threaded point of the catheter to the air.)

5. Rotate both wrists inward once more, and bring the catheter point and tube connector together, introduce the catheter into the connector, and immediately rotate away from you, screwing it tight.

6. At this point, the connection between the catheter and the infusion/drainage tube has been achieved, and you can proceed to the next stage (infusion or drainage).

Note: After pulling the pull ring off the end of the infusion/drainage tube and the iodine cap off the end of the catheter, connection should be made as quickly as possible, to reduce exposure to the air and keep the risk of infection to a minimum.

It took me four or five seconds to complete this stage, and in four years, I never had an accident.

家庭腹透最重要的一道工序
——腹腔管与灌入／引流管的連结

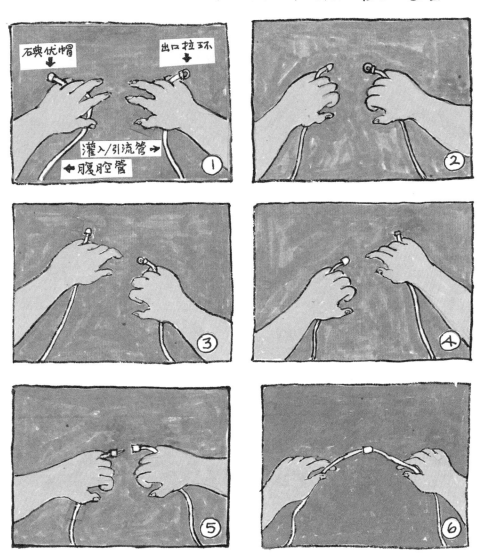

The most important stage in home dialysis: connecting the catheter to the infusion/drainage tube.

LABELS (CLOCKWISE FROM TOP LEFT) Iodine cap, pull ring, infusion/drainage tube, abdominal catheter

"去拿把剪刀来!我要把
这被子剪小一点!"

"Get me the scissors! I want to cut a bit off this quilt!"

"你故意把舒舒藏起来了……"

"You're deliberately hiding Shushu from me!"

In the early stages of Meitang's illness, she sometimes said things that just didn't follow, or that seemed unreasonable, or odd. I always put these down to the changes in temperament that were a normal part of the aging process. Then one day Meitang was lying in bed and suddenly said: "Get me the scissors, this quilt's too big, I want to cut a bit off it!" I was appalled: she really was becoming confused. At that instant, I felt lonelier than I had in decades.

Another day, Meitang and I were alone at home. About five o'clock in the afternoon, Meitang suddenly shouted for Shushu. Our granddaughter was still at work, and I told her so. But Meitang wouldn't believe me; she got up and searched every room in the house. When she didn't find her, she sat on the sitting room sofa and told me I was deliberately hiding Shushu from her. I realized that Meitang would never be her old self again, and the thought plunged me into despair. I sat weeping on the floor and phoned our children to ask them to come over.

美棠想吃杏花楼的马蹄蛋糕

Meitang wanted some water chestnut cakes from the Apricot Blossom patisserie.

One evening, Meitang suddenly said she'd love some water chestnut cakes from the Apricot Blossom patisserie. There was nowhere nearby that sold them, so I got on my bicycle and went some distance in search of them. Fortunately, although it was quite late by the time I got to the shop, I succeeded in buying some, but when I finally brought the cakes to her in bed, she did not want them. I was eighty-seven years old by then, and when our children found out, they all took me to task for going out on the bicycle at night. I should have known that their mother was confused. But I could never get out of the habit of doing as she asked me.

"我的那件黑底红花旗袍在哪里？"

"Where's my black qipao with the red flowers?"

On another occasion, Meitang asked me for her black qipao with the red flowers on it. But she didn't have a qipao like that. Perhaps she had had it once, and now this long-forgotten garment had floated up from the depths of her memory. I wondered whether we should get a tailor to make her another black qipao with red flowers and talked to our children about it. They were adamant that we should not. And exactly as they predicted, in no time at all, Meitang completely forgot the whole matter, and never mentioned it again.

"你不要乱吃东西啊！"

"Stop eating so much!"

One early evening Meitang suddenly called me into the bedroom and admonished me: "Stop eating so much, and stop riding that bicycle!" At that time, she looked just as calm and rational as she always had. However, she used to doze off once she had finished speaking, then wake up again, and come out with more strange things.

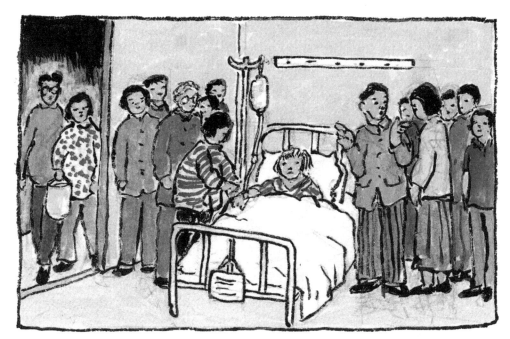

美棠住进了医院

Meitang was admitted to the hospital.

In the spring of 2008, Meitang's condition worsened, and finally she was admitted to the hospital. By then, she was constantly confused and agitated, rambling on and on. The hospital staff told us that she sang old songs, one after another.

The doctor prescribed hemodialysis for her, but she refused to cooperate and kept lifting her legs so that the procedure could not be carried out.

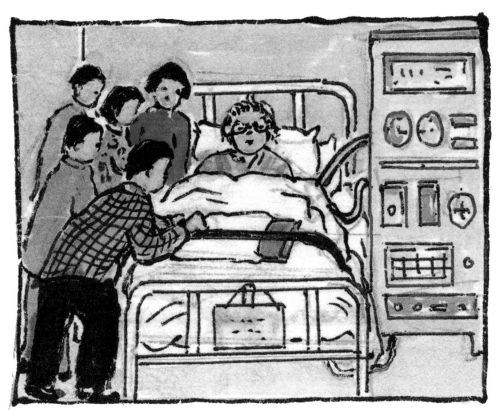

红木板 帮助做"血透"

Using a rosewood board to keep her legs still for the hemodialysis

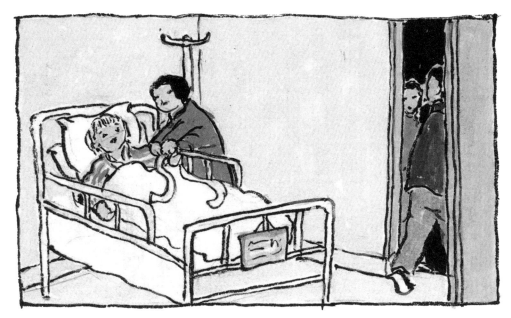

"莫绑我呀！莫绑我呀！"

"Don't tie me down! Don't tie me down!"

We all racked our brains about how to keep Meitang's legs down. My son-in-law, Zhang Weide, put a good deal of thought into this; he went home and found a fine piece of rosewood, enveloped it in layers of towels, and placed this on Meitang's knees. Then she was quiet.

We all of us grow old and die. However, we hoped that our small success with the rosewood plank might prove a good omen for Meitang's health.

By now, Meitang either slept all day or, when she did wake up, tried to pull all the tubes and needles out. This was very dangerous, and we were forced to ask the nursing staff to ensure that, at night, her hands were tied to the cot rails with gauze strips. Every time visiting hours were over and we were leaving, we would hear Meitang shouting: "Don't tie me down! Don't tie me down!" It was agonizing to listen to.

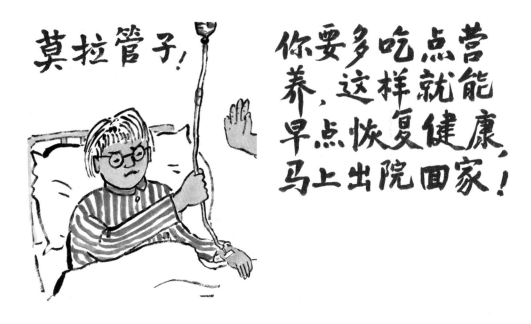

I used to communicate with Meitang mainly by writing notes or drawing pictures.

"Don't pull the tubes out!" "If you eat a bit more, you'll be better soon and can come home!"

Meitang became increasingly deaf and needed hearing aids, but as her illness worsened, she could no longer use them. I used to communicate with her mainly by writing notes or drawing pictures. Sometimes, when she looked at them, I got a response.

One day, when Yunhong was with her, Meitang suddenly woke up and seemed clear-headed. She said to our daughter: "You must make sure you look after your father properly!" Then she dozed off again.

In 2008, Chinese New Year's Eve fell on February 6. Our children had discussed having Meitang at home for the Spring Festival celebrations, and Maotou had borrowed a trundle bed from the hospital. The day before New Year's Eve, we brought her home. Lezeng set up the trundle bed on top of his big bed, and we arranged coat hangers and clothes airers on either side, with her tubes and syringes suspended from them. We spent the Spring Festival celebrations together with her, but she either dozed or was confused and agitated. This was not working, and on the eighth day of the New Year, we had to readmit her to the hospital.

"你要好好照顾你爸爸啊!"

"You must make sure you look after your father properly!"

It was hard to imagine that, after so many happy family gatherings and leave-takings we had had, there would one day be a final one.

On the morning of March 19, I went to the hospital to see Meitang. Yunhong was with me. At around ten o'clock, doctors and nurses rushed in to perform CPR on Meitang. Her eyes had been shut, but then they suddenly opened, and she looked around and caught sight of me standing behind the medical staff. I saw her right eye grow moist, and a tear slowly trickled from it. A few seconds later, she shut her eyes again; in spite of all the medics' efforts, they could not rouse her.

Around eleven, I saw she was sleeping peacefully and went home for a rest.

At three in the afternoon, Maotou and Yunhong hurried home to pick up a few clothes for Meitang and took me to the hospital. I stepped into the sickroom a little after four. She lay there as if fast asleep. I took her hand—it felt quite warm still, but gradually it became cold.

Meitang had left us. She was at peace. The children hovered outside the door, except for Guobin, who stayed with me. He told me that the exact time of death was 4:23 p.m.

When we were young and in love, we were never worried about providing for ourselves. Meitang often said that the two of us should find a quiet spot in the countryside, have a small allotment, and live the simple life. The dreams of starry-eyed youth. At the time, we had no idea that the old China of folk songs would soon be gone forever. We honestly believed that we could "buy a homestead with ten mu of garden, and grow melons and vegetables . . . making do with simple clothes and food and living out our days, with no need for distant travels," as Shen Fu describes it.[30]

最后的
一滴眼
泪

2012.6.29

A last tear

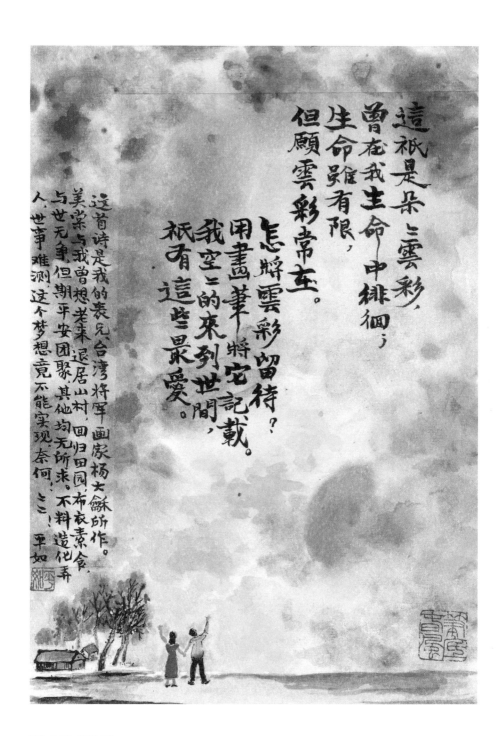

這祇是朵三雲彩，
曾在我生命中徘徊；
生命雖有限，
但願雲彩常在。

怎將雲彩留待？
用畫筆將它記載。
我空二的來列世間，
祇有這些景愛。

这首诗是我的表兄，台湾将军画家杨大勲所作。美棠与我曾想老来退居山村，回归田园，布衣素食，与世无争，但期平安团聚，其他均无所求。不料造化弄人，世事难测，这个梦想竟不能实现，奈何！二二 平如

In middle age, we two were parted and the family faced much hardship. Meitang used to implore me to take care of my health. She said that once the children were independent, she would come and live with me in Anhui. "If we're in good health, then when we're old, we can go out for walks, see a few films, buy ourselves something nice to eat. That would be wonderful." That was the kind of woman she was, innocent and fun-loving, asking little from life. What kept her going during the decades of hard work was the thought that one day we would be able to live in peace and happiness.

And, late in our lives, things did settle down. Heaven must have been watching over me, because I survived two major operations and made a full recovery. It was Meitang who became ill. She was worn down by years of chronic kidney disease, a poor diet, and increasing immobility. Her wishes were so simple, yet remained unfulfilled. "Other lives we cannot divine, this life is finished."[31] And lamenting over it is fruitless!

On March 23, 2008, Meitang's funeral was held at the Longhua Funeral Home. I wrote this poem of lament:

We endured the most difficult of times, and gradually our lives became better.
  But heaven granted us so few years together and today I grieve bitterly,
  because now you are gone.
Who can anticipate the vicissitudes of life? I have been through good times and bad,
  and am disillusioned with this earthly world. I long only to be reunited with you
  in the next life.

"Memories, like clouds of many hues / Hover over me / Every life has a term, yet / I wish I could keep those memories forever. / How to keep them always with me? / Record them in words and pictures. / I came into this world empty-handed / Only these have I truly loved."

This poem was written by my cousin Yang Dahe, a Taiwan army general and painter. Meitang and I had dreamed of moving to the countryside when we retired, to live the simple life, to remove ourselves from world affairs, to live together in peace and make no demands of anyone. But fate plays cruel tricks on us humans, life moves in mysterious ways, and we were unable to fulfill our dream. Alas!

The Passing of the Seasons

(Meitang's letters, 1973–1978)

TELEGRAM ON LEFT "Dear Pingru: I got your telegram yesterday, the tenth, so I'm not worried anymore. Your letter dated the eighteenth arrived on the twenty-first of March, but then nothing. I wrote on the twenty-third but still no reply, so I was worried. Since the first of this month, I've been hoping for a letter every day. Maotou wrote to you on the fourth and didn't hear from you either. I was frantic with worry. On the eighth, I even left work at midday to see if there was any news, and there wasn't, or at 6:30 p.m. either, when I came home. I wanted to make a long-distance call because you would definitely not be in the factory in the evening. Then the children suggested sending a telegram and that's what we did, because there's never been such a long gap in your letters before. Then yesterday we got your letter of the eighth, and today your letter of the fifth finally came, but the ten yuan you said you sent never arrived, nor your letter of the twenty-eighth. I don't know why. Why did your letter of the fifth only come today? The Liu An postmark is not very clear but it looks like it was sent on the ninth, and the money hasn't arrived at all. I don't know if you sent it yourself or gave it to someone to mail, if so, you could ask them. It's very strange. When we didn't get your letters of the twenty-eighth and the fifth, we were really worried that something might have happened to you, and the one from the twenty-eighth still hasn't turned up. I was worried about two things: (1) maybe you'd fainted from the paint fumes or (2) there had been an accident when you got to Liu An in the evening and crossed on the ferry, and the more I thought about it . . ."

TELEGRAM ON RIGHT "To: Rao Pingru, Assembly Workshop, Liu An Car Parts Factory. No letter for long time, reply telegram, Meitang."

May 30, morning

Dear Pingru,

. . .

Xizeng has a day off today and has taken Lezeng to see a film called *Acrobatics*. It's really good; if they put it on near you, you should go and see it. It's impossible to get tickets in Shanghai, but Xizeng's work held a raffle and he got two tickets. Then there's the documentary *The Twenty-seventh Session of the UN,* which I hear is also very good.

. . . When will you be back in Shanghai? Why not come back for the Midautumn Festival? Lezeng will be staying through the hot weather. The farmwork in Jiangxi is tiring and he needs a break. He hasn't been back in Shanghai in the hot weather for years, and spends every day indoors, practicing his calligraphy and ink-brush painting.

June 5 is the Dragon Boat Festival. We got 1.5 jin of glutinous rice per person and half a jin of red beans per household. Guobin brought another half a jin of glutinous rice and we plan to make the whole lot into zongzi dumplings. We didn't make any last year, but this year Lezeng is with us, which doesn't happen often. Since the children got sent away to work, we hardly ever get a chance to be together. So I'm going to make some meat zongzi because they don't like the sweet ones, except for Maotou. The rest of us prefer meat zongzi. I'll get everything ready on June 1 and Maotou gets here on Saturday, June 2. He won't be here on the day itself, but that doesn't matter. We'll celebrate a couple of days early. Do they sell zongzi in your canteen? For the past dozen years, you haven't been able to celebrate with us. It's hard for people living away to get home for special occasions.

. . .

Maotou says he's taken his exams and got good marks, over 90 percent in all of them. He wrote you a letter for me to post but he never told me where he had put it when he left, and now I can't find it.

Time to go to work now, I'll be in touch soon!

All my best,

Meitang

July 8

Dear Pingru,

I've just received your letter. It's good news that you're coming back to Shanghai in August; the children are delighted. If you're bringing some cooking oil what will you bring it in? If it's too awkward, bring just a small amount. Don't bother with the ground sesame seed, we already have several jin of it. It's nice to have things like that at New Year, but not good to eat too many sweets normally. . . . Buy a set of casseroles instead, I can't buy them here, all the ones we had are broken, and we haven't got any for the Spring Festival. A set of four would be good, don't spend more than three yuan.

. . .

The children are saying they're going to buy you a short-sleeved shirt that will be comfortable for you to wear when you get back, because you don't have one. Would you like white or pale gray?

We're all fine, don't worry!

All my best,

Meitang

❋

July 26, noon

Dear Pingru,

Your letter arrived. Which day are you setting off? The children can go and meet you at the station. Anything you can't buy, don't worry about it.

Yunhong has been asking if you can get pumpkin. If you can, will you buy her some?

. . .

Maotou is interning at the hospital and says he keeps having to ask people the time. He says it's really annoying, and when he's completed his six months next year, he's going to get Xizeng to buy a watch from his savings and lend it to him. We really haven't got a bean to rub together but there is nothing we can do. The last dozen years, the children have grown up and all have things they want to do, and we've been scraping the bottom of the barrel. . . .

Shanghai has been very hot for the last few days, but the evenings are cooler. Watermelon is nine cents a jin, I didn't buy any.

First, I didn't have the money, and second, I'd rather wait until you're back and we can all have a bit more to eat. Lezeng hasn't had watermelon for years, they don't have it in Jiangxi, or only in the city and it's very expensive. They don't have that sort of money, and, anyway, they're too far from the city to go and buy it. Anyway, we'll wait till you're back and we can all enjoy it together. That's all for now. We can talk more when you're back!

All my best,

Meitang

❋

Morning of September 8

Dear Pingru,

You left two weeks ago, it's gone really fast. The weather has got cooler and it's the Midautumn Festival on the eleventh. Buy yourself something nice to eat! And we'll do the same. Yunhong is getting over her cold. Yesterday I sent a package to Guobin with some rubber shoes. I got someone to buy some salt fish and some mooncakes for him. I felt much better after I sent it off. He can't get back but at least I sent him something nice to eat.

. . .

I'll write more soon!

All my best,

Meitang

❋

September 17

Dear Pingru,

I received both your letters. . . .

We had a good Midautumn Festival. I bought about a jin of pork, and steamed it with rice noodles. Mrs. Zhu sent us some mooncakes as a present, so we ate those and didn't need to buy any. I was happy to hear that you had duck. Maotou was surprised duck is so cheap where you are. He says, "Tell Dad not to buy peanuts next time he comes, buy a duck for us!"

He's right, that's cheap; in Shanghai a duck that big would cost at least four yuan. But it will be difficult to bring a duck with you, better wait until the weather's colder. Then if you come, you can have it killed the day before and hang it on the line to dry out, then bring it in a nylon bag the next day. But you don't have to. We can get ducks in Shanghai, it's just that they're pricey.

. . . Maotou is still worried about starting his internship after the Spring Festival, because everyone's got a watch, or they borrow one from their brother or sister. What am I to do? If I could get hold of the money I'd get him one, he needs it at the hospital. I'll stop now, as I have to go to work.

All my best,

Meitang

(Forget the duck, it's too difficult. The children just say the first thing that comes into their heads. If you can get sesame oil, bring a jin of that.)

❀

December 10

Dear Pingru,

I received your letters with the six yuan and the twenty yuan. Here's some good news! Yunhong heard today that she's been offered a job at the Shanghai Yangtze Calligraphy Engravers. They come under the Shanghai Municipal Handicrafts Bureau, they're just a collective but big, almost as good as being in a state-owned enterprise. . . . She doesn't know yet which workshop she'll be sent to, but it's the ideal job for her. . . .

I just received your last letter. You must be missing my letters! This one should cheer you up. The Calligraphy Engravers belong to the Fine Arts and Handicrafts Company. That's all for now.

All my best,

Meitang

"Yearning for you, I start to think the ocean's not deep at all."—Bai Juyi
Pingru, the fifth month of the year Ren Chen (2012), the twenty-ninth year of the Chinese sixty-year cycle

January 10

Dear Pingru,

I'm sending this package with someone.

. . .

Yunhong works long hours; sometimes they have meetings and she doesn't get home till after six. Her workshop produces calligraphy model books. She has to write the characters both ways, right way around, and back to front for making the engravings. They produce small notebooks too. She practices her calligraphy every day, and brings work home with her too. So she has no time for housework. Lezeng did a big spring clean on his own today, and then on Sunday, Yunhong has a day off, and we'll unpick the quilt undercovers and wash them for New Year.

Last month I sent Guobin a jin of peanuts and a jin of salt fish. Last time he left, he didn't take his padded jacket so Maotou's been wearing it because he doesn't have one. I know Guobin's got only a really old padded jacket in Jiangxi, so I wrote and asked if he wanted me to send his good one, but he said no, let Maotou wear it. I'm worried because the weather's turned so cold, so I sent him a padded waistcoat and put the peanuts and fish in with it. . . .

It hasn't been at all cold in Shanghai and it hasn't rained for three months either. The weather forecast says it'll rain tomorrow. Xizeng bought you a hat today, it's a good one. Your ears won't get cold because you can pull the flaps down.

All my best,

Meitang

❄

January 13

Dear Pingru,

Your letter and the money arrived.

. . .

We haven't bought our New Year's food yet, we're waiting until Xizeng gets his wages and bonus. Yunhong gets hers on the fifteenth. She always gives me 10 yuan and keeps 7.8 yuan back for food and bits and pieces. People think we're quite well off but actually we're just scraping by. The kids are grown up now, it's not like when they were little; they need proper clothes and we need things for the house too. Every month I try to make ends meet, but I never do. But our children are good to me. Yesterday, a woman in our workshop was crying and telling us how she'd had several children and they were very poor. Her kids are older than ours, and they've had jobs for a long time, but they don't give their parents a cent from their wages. Her husband is ill and his sick pay is only fifty yuan a month, not enough to get by. Their kids have watches and bicycles, and the family's always arguing about money. This Spring Festival, her husband tried to get the kids to cough up a bit extra, and got into a terrible row with them.

We're fine, we'll have a happy Spring Festival. I'll buy meat, fish, and with your two chickens, we'll be fine. . . . But will you have enough for yourself? You need something to eat too.

That's all for now.

Have a happy New Year!
Meitang

※

January 24

Dear Pingru,

Today's the second day of the lunar New Year. We cooked a big dinner on the last day of the old year. Your two chickens were big and fat, we ate them cold. The children said they would have been even better if they'd been fresh and we could have made chicken soup from them. When you come for the next New Year, bring a couple of live chickens with you and then we can make soup. Then we had the soybeans you brought last time you came, we made them into a soup with pigs' trotters. It was delicious. The children said they had never had such good soybean soup, really thick . . . and yesterday we had four cold dishes: a bit more than a quarter of a brined chicken; a dish of soy sauce–stewed beef and smoked fish, half and half; roasted gluten and peanuts with daylilies and wood-ear mushrooms; and a dish of shredded daikon radish and jellyfish in scallion oil. Then we had four stir-fried dishes: sliced pork and water chestnuts, "clam eggs"—that's minced pork and bean sprouts, you beat four eggs, fry half the mixture in a pan, add the minced meat, then the rest

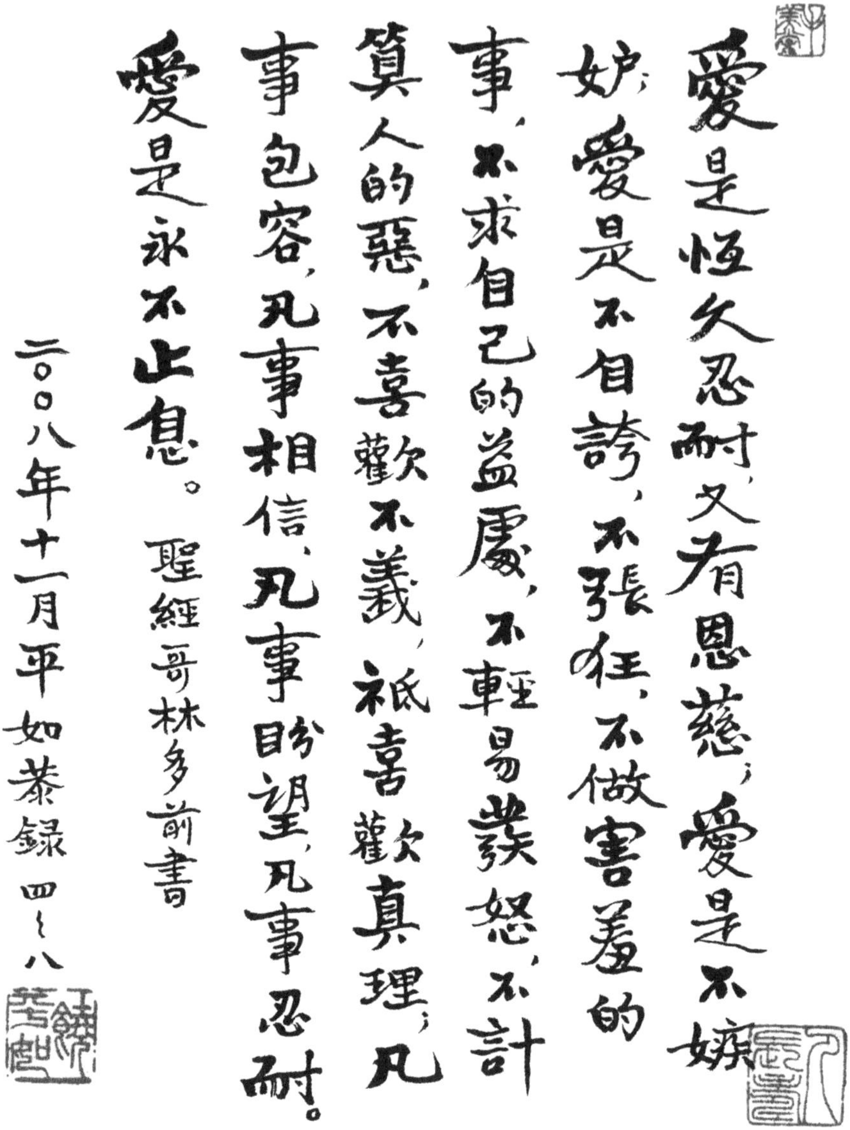

愛是恆久忍耐，又有恩慈；愛是不嫉妒；愛是不自誇，不張狂，不做害羞的事，不求自己的益處，不輕易發怒，不計算人的惡，不喜歡不義，祇喜歡真理；凡事包容，凡事相信，凡事盼望，凡事忍耐。愛是永不止息。

聖經哥林多前書

二〇〇八年十一月平如恭錄 四～八

"Love is patient, love is kind and is not jealous; love does not brag and is not arrogant, does not act unbecomingly; it does not seek its own, is not provoked, does not take into account a wrong suffered, does not rejoice in unrighteousness, but rejoices with the truth. Love bears all things, believes all things, hopes all things, endures all things. Love never fails."
—From the First Epistle of St. Paul to the Corinthians, 13:4–8

of the beaten egg, and so it looks like a big filled dumpling, or a large "clam." Then we had fish slices in vinegar, sweet and sour pork ribs, some side dishes, and stir-fried rice noodles. And we had red-cooked fish, red-cooked pork, and the pigs' trotter soup. And two jin of wine.

Yunhong has engraved a character and is sending it for you to see. It's good that now she can do her own calligraphy and engraving.

It's very noisy in the house now that we have a radio. There are lots of New Year's programs, and the crosstalk comedy sketches are very good. The children shut the door in the evenings and play poker and listen to the radio. They have a great time. My mother and I lie in bed listening. The kids are saying that their granny will be eighty years old on the twenty-seventh of the twelfth lunar month this year. Guobin will be back and you too, and we will have a really happy New Year. . . .

We're fine. Everyone says that Yunhong and I have put on weight. But Xizeng's gotten thinner. Maotou is thin too, but his color is better.

Did you get out for New Year's? It's rained every day in Shanghai, but it hasn't rained for several months so we needed it.

That's enough for now, I'll write more soon.

All my best!

Meitang

❋

February 11

Dear Pingru,

Your letter of February 2 arrived.

. . .

Xizeng has had high blood pressure and feels dizzy. Maotou made him go and get it checked out. It turns out it's a kidney problem. His urine protein was 2+ and he's got a week off work. The doctor keeps giving him sick leave, but he never takes it, because if you have more than five days off sick in a month you lose all of your five-yuan bonus and they dock another 2.5 yuan off your wages every day.

With the last few days off work, he says his wages will be down next month. I said his health's important so we'll just have to put up with it. . . . The day before yesterday I made soybean and pork ribs soup and made him eat a bit more, but I couldn't give it all to him, there are other mouths to feed, what can I do?

. . . I haven't had a letter from Guobin for ages, I don't know why. I miss his letters. Someone else wrote saying they're all in debt this year so he has no money to come home and is too depressed to write. When are you coming back? If you come, there might not be any need to borrow money, we're actually much better off now than the last couple of years, and one extra mouth to feed is nothing. In March we get our clothing coupons, you should use your book-buying money on an unpadded quilt, and keep it for yourself. You can't get anything in Shanghai even for ten yuan. Bring some cotton batting when you come, and we can pad up your old one and you can put it on the bed and sleep on top of it, that way you won't be cold. You can't go on suffering these hardships.

. . . It's past nine o'clock, so that's all till next time.

All my best,

Meitang

✳

February 27, evening

Dear Pingru,

I didn't get your letter of the sixteenth until the twenty-fourth. It took so long, I've been so looking forward to it. You're all on your own so if I don't hear from you I can't help worrying that you've fallen sick. The children were wondering why they hadn't heard from you too. But we're not worried anymore.

. . .

That's good that you're coming back in April. What a pity that Lezeng will be leaving in March so you won't see him. He's planning to leave in the middle of the month and I've borrowed twenty yuan from the community workshop and another twenty from the credit union, to be paid back in installments. He and Guobin both need cotton shirts. And there's soap to buy and other necessities, and food for Guobin, of course. The money is never enough . . . the kids are grown up now, they need more clothes. Lezeng's sweatshirt is really old. I said we'd better buy another one, but he said: "No, don't, no one wears sweatshirts anymore; the next time I get something, I want a sweater."

He's right that no one in Shanghai wears sweatshirts anymore, and last year Guobin said he wanted a sweater too. I feel so sorry for the kids. Everyone has a sweater nowadays, but they can't afford one . . .

There's been heavy snow in Shanghai in the last few days, and it's terribly cold. But it must be even colder where you are, and especially for you, you haven't got a decent quilt, or padded jacket. Come what may, we're got to buy you new ones! Xizeng went to see the doctor today. He's still on sick leave and his blood pressure is 150 over 90, mainly because of his kidney infection. These chronic infections are very troublesome. Maotou says there's no definitive cure.

Well, that's enough for now, I'll write again soon.

All my best!

Meitang

March

Dear Pingru,

Your letter arrived, and the fifteen yuan.

. . . Yesterday the letter you sent with Mr. Zhu arrived. I didn't want him to bring it over in this hot weather, so I waited till evening and asked Xizeng and Maotou to go and pick it up. . . . Mr. Zhu says they told him you've not been well, you keep fainting. I was so worried and upset. What's the problem? Have you been to see a doctor? What did they say? Is it benzene poisoning from the paint fumes? Or are you run-down? But anyway, this problem must have been brewing for quite some time, you've had such a hard life and such poor food for years, I'm sure that's the reason. From now on, you're not to give your food coupons to anyone else, eat all that food yourself. And you're not to save your coupons and bring food home. . . . Mr. Zhu's better at looking after himself than you are, and we've got plenty to eat at home, we have a meat dish at dinner every day. Guobin and Lezeng work very hard, but they're young, and they can stand it better. You're the one I'm most worried about; you're getting old, it's not surprising you haven't been well. The paint shop wouldn't give you an allowance for nutritional supplements unless you were in poor health, would they?

Mr. Zhu says that even though you're doing the bookkeeping, they keep paint in your office and that can't be good for you. And on top of that, you do an extra half day of laboring. Now that's enough; if there isn't any overtime, then so be it. I've always been worried about you doing that work. The supplements allowance is only given in serious cases, and then you give it to someone else, and don't eat yourself, of course you're going to be run-down!

. . . Maotou will be assigned a job at the end of this year, so we'll be a bit better off. So starting in August, you can send us five yuan less out of your monthly wages. You absolutely must take those supplements. I know my health isn't good, but my dizzy spells stopped years ago, and it was never as bad as the fainting you've had. And you're all alone with no one to look after you. You absolutely, absolutely must take care of yourself! What I want to do, when I retire, is go and live with you for a bit. We've had such hard lives for all these years, and we deserve a bit of a rest. But what's the point if we're in poor health? It would be so sad if we were ill all the time. If we're in good health, then when we're old, we can go out for walks, see a few films, buy ourselves something nice to eat. That would be wonderful. The children are grown up, I don't want to go on living with them forever. They'll have their own homes, they won't need us to look after them, we should look after each other. It would be so sad if we were ill. So you really must take care, don't skip meals, be more like Mr. Zhu, cook yourself something good, and live a bit better. Food hall meals are no good. "Hall" is a nice name, but the meals are not good value.

I felt a little heavy-headed today and went and got my blood pressure taken. It was 68 over 92, and the doctor told me this is low. I remember yours was 70 over 90, and that's on the low side too. It's all a sign of being run-down. People of our age should be 80 over 130. But we eat meat every day, don't worry about us, just look after yourself!

Meitang

※

April 28

Dear Pingru,

I got your letter yesterday, so I know you arrived safely. . . .

Lezeng has decided to leave on May 2 and is going to buy his ticket the day after tomorrow, the thirtieth. There's no point him hanging around. . . . Once he has the ticket, we'll cable Guobin to go and meet him.

Parting is always sad when we've had good times together. Even though I know you'll all be back at New Year, I still find it hard.

. . .

Lezeng put those two apples into your bag. When the children read in your letter that you didn't get dinner, they were upset with you for not taking some snacks with you and having to go hungry.

. . . Yesterday I made some fried fish floss for Lezeng and went to bed late. So I'm having an early night tonight, and I'll stop now.

All my best,
Meitang

❋

May 19

Dear Pingru,

Your letter arrived several days ago (on the twelfth). Lately, the weather has been warming up, so I washed all our winter clothes and hung them out to air. Yesterday it was thirty degrees, and I took a bath and washed the clothes. . . .

Lezeng has written. The day he arrived, Guobin and two classmates went to meet him. But the train was late; it didn't arrive till eight o'clock when it should have gotten there at six. On their way from the station, it poured with rain, and by the time they got there, he was exhausted. It's on top of a high mountain, a steep climb, and with the suitcases too. They were wading through mud, it was very hard going. I couldn't bear to think of it. . . . Lezeng says that Guobin and the others are very busy. They go out to work as soon as it gets light, then come back for breakfast at half past eight. If the weather's good and the sky's clear, then they'll do a night shift by moonlight. They don't even have time to wash their clothes.

. . . Maotou will be back at the end of the month. He's still so skinny.

We're fine, don't worry about us, you take care of yourself, I'll write more soon.

All my best,

Meitang

(This is a seal that Yunhong carved for Guobin.)

❋

November 2

Dear Pingru,

Your letter arrived. Some things Maotou already told you about in his letter. . . .

Maotou had a week off work with a lung infection. It started when he had a pain in the left side of his chest, and when he had an X-ray, there was a shadow on his lung. The doctor said it was viral pneumonia and prescribed ten bottles of penicillin and fourteen bottles of streptomycin. He has injections morning and evening, so he can hardly walk now. In a week, he has another X-ray and we hope it isn't TB. These past few mornings, his temperature has been 38.5, and by the afternoon it's down to 37.4. I've been very worried. What if he still has an infection at the time he's assigned a job? Maotou's never had a good appetite, and mentally he seems exhausted; I've been worried about him for a while. I just haven't been able to buy him nutritious food. It's bad enough that Xizeng is ill, and now another one's sick, I've been frantic with worry. The last couple of days, Xizeng and Maotou have been drinking the milk between them, and I bought a bit of pork to make soup, and some fruit too. Each family in Shanghai is allowed to buy a jin of eggs every month so I've been bringing some home for him. Last month, Xizeng bought Maotou a jin and half of wool out of his wages, for a sweater. He said a woolen sweater is cooler, it's too early to wear a padded jacket. And Yunhong is knitting the sweater for him. . . .

The weather's getting cooler, you take care of yourself, I'm keeping my eye on you. In our community workshop, people sometimes take on extra jobs, but I won't be applying, first because I don't think I'm up to it and second because the children are not well and I'd worry if I was working longer hours. . . .

Yunhong carved a stamp for Xizeng's friend Qin, and Xizeng's going to give it to her on his day off.

She's done one for Maotou too, you can see it here. Maotou's is made of ox bone, and Qin's is made of white Perspex. . . .

I need to go to a meeting now, I'll write more soon.

All my best,

Meitang

※

November 10

Dear Pingru,

I was just going to write to you when I got your letter of the sixth. I'm so glad to hear that you've bought an unpadded quilt and some long johns. I'm very relieved. When you come back this year, bring a length of cotton batting, to pad out the old stuff. And we'll buy you a new quilt top cover. Little by little, we'll get there!

. . .

Maotou is much better. He had an X-ray the day before yesterday and it was clear. But he's had a rash all over his body the last few days. He's still rather low, I don't know why. The last couple of days I bought meat for them. They're not as healthy as I am. Now it's me that has to do all the shopping and empty the rubbish, either because they're too busy, or they're sick, so it's best for me to do it.

. . . We're fine, don't worry. More soon.

All my best,

Meitang

※

August 3

Dear Pingru,

I got your letter of July 30. We've had thunderstorms in Shanghai the last few days, and that brought cooler weather, though it began to get hotter again yesterday.

The eighth is the Start of Autumn, so the heat can't go on much longer. When it cools down and work is less busy, we won't feel so tired from the heat.

. . .

In the *Wenhui News* of July 13, there was an article about the Jiangxi Huaguo Mountains.[32] That's right where Guobin and Lezeng are, in Yichun prefecture. If your work gets the *Wenhui News,* borrow it and take a look. We've got a new young worker in our community workshop, she's from Guobin's commune. . . . She says none of the sent-down city youth want to be sent to the Huaguo Mountains because life is too hard there. They work all day and all night and hardly get any sleep. It's so good of Guobin to take the lead and volunteer for the hard jobs. Their leader refused them leave to come back last year, but maybe this year he can come with the other sent-down youth and they can have a good time in Shanghai.

. . .

I've got to go to work now, I started my letter early this morning because there was a cool breeze. We're fine, don't worry about us!

All my best,

Meitang

(Xizeng has bought you three books, on Chinese literature and tai chi. The next time someone comes to Shanghai, they can take them back to you.)

✳

Dear Pingru,

. . .

Yesterday I put in some hours at the mooncakes factory. It's hard work and a lot of stress. I did overtime too, so I worked from seven in the morning till half past nine at night. It was after ten before I got home. Besides that, I was up at two in the morning to go and queue up for food, and at six o'clock, when I'd done all the cooking, I took the number 16 bus to Xinya Bridge, got off, and walked the last part. I got only half an hour for lunch, so it's been a hard day. I came home, and bathed and washed the clothes. The market was incredibly noisy today too, so I've got a terrible headache. I'm on a late shift, from two in the afternoon until eleven at night, so I'll finish this letter and have a nap, otherwise I won't last. I still need to buy eggs, which I didn't get this morning.

Maotou starts his shift at midday today and he's having his lunch before he goes, so I'd better stop.

All my best,

Meitang

P.S. I'm enclosing twenty-six jin of food coupons.

*

October 5, midday

Dear Pingru,

I got your letter and the ten yuan. I've taken on some extra jobs so I haven't had a moment to spare, and also Cousin Zhang's come from Yunnan to stay for five days and I've had to take her shopping. It's exhausting. The job at the mooncakes factory stops at the end of the month. It's really hard work. I weighed myself and I've lost six jin. I've sprained a muscle too, from having to carry metal trays around. At the start, I was all right, but the last couple of days I've had a pain on the right-hand side of my chest and it's hard to breathe. I saw the doctor today and she put some ointment on it. Old people are useless. So now, even though the building site is recruiting laborers, I'm not going. I heard they don't want anyone over fifty, and I'm not up to it anyway.

. . . The extra jobs earned me fourteen yuan, which just about got us through the holiday and meant I could entertain our visitors, but I've been exhausted for a month. Xizeng says: "I told you not to go!"

Maotou is still expecting to be assigned a job at the end of the year, but nothing's settled yet. . . . Yesterday, a lot of his classmates came around and they all had watches and leather shoes. Their teacher told Maotou: "Everyone else looks like a proper doctor, it's only you who still looks like a student." I told him to tell her: "I *am* a student!" But Maotou said she'd take offense.

I took a day off today and now I'm going to bed. I'll write more soon!

All my best,

Meitang

October 8

Dear Pingru,

I got your letter of the fourth. And today a letter came from Guobin . . . in it, he says he's got a girlfriend. Who is she? Tell me when you come back. Imagine him getting a girlfriend! In the letter, he asks us to buy him a pair of wool pants and leather shoes. . . .

We had a good National Day this year. We bought pork, beef, tripe, and pig's tongue, and my sister gave us some mooncakes. I'm sure our dinner was as good as yours. You must look after yourself, now that the weather's getting colder, you must buy that quilt liner. In your letter, you said twelve feet, but that's not enough, you generally need eighteen feet, because the fabric's narrow, so you need three lengths sewn together to get the width. Whatever you do, make sure you buy enough. You can't base it on the size of your old quilt, because the new one will have thicker batting in it.

The last few days in Shanghai, it's rained every day and it's getting cooler too. You make sure you don't get caught by the drop in temperature. We can look after ourselves, we're fine, don't worry.

All my best,
Meitang

❋

June 30, afternoon

Dear Pingru,

. . .

I don't want you to send twenty-five yuan next month. You won't have any left to buy food with. We'll think of another way. Send twenty yuan like before. It's important to look after your health. Today I bought some pork to make sea kelp soup for Xizeng, and we got some fish too. We have a meat dish every day . . . but I don't think you do! Tomatoes are cheap now, six cents a jin in Shanghai, you should buy some and eat them like fruit, they're good for you. But if you're going to eat them raw, you need good-quality tomatoes. If they're too soft, they're not nice, they should be red but still firm.

It's cooler again today, it rained. Make sure you're wearing enough and look after your health. We're fine, don't worry.

Meitang

Morning of September 4

Dear Pingru,

I got your letter. I'm in better health than before, because I'm getting more food. I got a sore throat because of my nerves. I don't eat anything spicy nowadays. . . .

Guobin is so different from Xizeng, he can't give up the cigarettes; Lezeng gives him ten yuan a month when he can, even though he earns only a bit more than twenty a month himself. Guobin's girlfriend, Peizhi, sometimes gives him money too. I've asked him several times to cut down on the smoking. He won't be earning as much as the pocket money you get from now on, and then what will he do? He's getting older, what will he do when he marries? If Lezeng gets a university place, he won't have any spare cash himself. He says he'll give him some after he's graduated. The trouble is, Guobin's used to pleasing himself after all these years in the countryside, and that's hard to change.

. . .

I watched a Yugoslav film, it was very exciting. Xizeng's almost paid off the TV now. When you come back, you can watch it. The screen's a bit less than nine inches, but it's fine if you're just watching at home. We're not going to buy a wooden cabinet for it because we want to buy a twelve-inch. Only at the moment, customs is not letting in the CRT tubes for twelve-inch TVs. As soon as they do, we'll swap the nine-inch for a twelve-inch.

It would be so good if you could sort out your problem. If you could come back to Shanghai, that would be ideal. . . . We had several days of rain so it was nice and cool, but yesterday and today it was hot again. Is your back better? Look after yourself!

All my best,

Meitang

September 10, noon

Dear Pingru,

I got your letter on the fifth. . . . I've been terribly busy lately. Mother fell in her room. It was about eight in the evening of the sixth, and too late to take her to the hospital. She was in terrible pain and couldn't move so she groaned all night. We none of us could sleep, and we had to help her onto a potty whenever she needed to go. The next morning, Maotou went and borrowed a stretcher from the hospital and a bicycle and trailer from Xizeng's factory, and he and I, and the Fangs' son, got her onto the stretcher and onto the trailer, to take her to the hospital. We had to take her on the stretcher because she couldn't move. The hospital took an X-ray and said she'd broken her hip. She's going to need three months' bedrest. Luckily, Maotou's staying at home to look after her as we have to go to work. I come back twice a day to help her onto the potty. Maotou can't do that on his own, he can't move her. Maotou sleeps in her room at night and talks to her because she can't sleep. Maotou's lost a lot of weight in the last few days; he has to cook during the day, and look after her, and he doesn't get a good night's sleep either, but there's nothing we can do. I'm poorly too. I sleep in the next-door room and I'm disturbed by her moans and groans. I'm frantic with worry, she's so old, what can we do? We weren't prepared for this. . . .

The walnuts you bought us, I'll give them to Mother. If you can get any more, you eat them yourself. They say they're good for the lower back and hips. They're supposed to be steeped in rice wine. You chop up the kernels, and steam them with some sugar. Then you take a spoonful every day, in a cup of rice wine. It improves the circulation, so buy some for yourself too. Look after yourself. More news soon.

All my best,
Meitang

❋

October 10

Dear Pingru,

Your letter and the money arrived. We bought pork and a duck for National Day too, but duck without chicken and pickled goose is no good, it's all skin and no meat. I had three days off, I can't remember what I did, it's all been and gone now.

. . .

Mother is much better, I'm so relieved. She still can't get out of bed, though, she still has to have bedrest.

Old Mrs. L, who lives in this building, died a few days ago. She had a heart attack, mainly because the family had a big fight and that set it off. . . . The neighbors all sent wreaths, and so did we. They held the funeral at the Longhua Funeral Home. I didn't go, but Maotou went, and helped out. That was because Maotou used to take her to the doctor (her own family didn't do that). Poor woman.

. . . More soon!

All my best,

Meitang

※

November 10, morning

Dear Pingru,

Your letter arrived. Yesterday I got a letter from Lezeng too. He wants to take the exams for the Academy of Art, but it's not going to be easy, because he has to pass exams in Chinese language, politics, and math as well. He never had much formal schooling, but he might as well try. . . .

. . .

Today, your letter of November seventh arrived before I mailed this one. I'm glad you've sent Lezeng some painting materials; I sent him some painting paper and a drawing pad and a brush.

Even if your back's a bit better, you still need to look after it. Your padded jacket isn't enough in cold weather. You must get a new one made as soon as you get your wages. When it gets even colder, you can wear the padded waistcoat as well. Yunhong's nearly finished knitting the sweater for you. As soon as it's done, she'll get it off to you.

You said in your letter you want to become an English teacher. Let's see what happens. It would be best if you could come back to Shanghai, otherwise we'll have to keep writing.

Why don't you watch some films when you've got nothing else to do? I don't watch many, I can't be bothered. But I did watch *Commissioner Lin and the Opium War* on TV.[33]

We're fine, don't worry. Now it's getting colder, the most important thing is for you to look after yourself.

All my best,

Meitang

(Lezeng's got to take exams in humanities if he wants to get into the Academy of Arts. You should write him some study notes.)

Christmas Day, December 25

Dear Pingru,

The registered letter and two other letters all arrived, one after the other.

Time's going by fast. One more month and you'll be back. . . .

Xizeng's TV will be fixed soon and we can watch on New Year's Day. The children are excited because the New Year's Day programs are very good. There will be films like *Struggles in an Ancient City, Satisfied or Not?, Sentinel Under the Neon Lights,* and Kunqu Opera.[34] The movie theaters are expensive and it's hard to get tickets. Now we can watch them in our own home, even Mother enjoys them. So every evening, no one wants to do any work, we all sit around the TV. . . .

It's really cold in Shanghai. It's going to be minus 3 or 4 tomorrow. You look after yourself. Keep well!

Meitang

January 1, 1978, New Year's Day

Dear Pingru,

I received your letter of December 25. I sent you one the same day, you should have received it.

Today's New Year's Day. I'm on duty at the neighborhood phone kiosk in the morning and I have the afternoon off. We haven't been able to get hold of much food,

I just bought a jin of pork to make jiaozi dumplings. It's Yunhong's birthday today. We haven't bought her a present, but she likes eggs, so I'll buy some tomorrow. I haven't had a spare moment these last few days. I've had to do two hours overtime every evening, because we've got production targets.

We can watch Xizeng's TV now, and we've been watching every evening. Yesterday we watched till eleven at night (there were programs till 1:00 a.m. because of New Year's).

There were performances from film stars like Wang Danfeng, Huang Zongying, Bai Yang, and Qin Yi. . . . The neighbors all came around to watch. Our neighbors, Er Mao's family, hardly ever go to the movies; they like watching at our place.

I'll stop now and make the jiaozi. The kids won't move from in front of the TV.

All my best,

Meitang

March 26

Dear Pingru,

I got your letter, and all your news.

We're fine. Yesterday we watched *The Woman Messenger*. It was pretty good. The last few days we've seen the comedians Yao Mushuang and Zhou Bochun too.[35] The movies are always sold out and you can't get tickets even if you queue up at midnight. The day before yesterday they had *Everything in the Garden's Lovely* and *Satisfied or Not?* on the TV. The films are so-so but the actors are good, and we had a full house at home as well.

. . .

We hope so much that you can transfer back to Shanghai. Everything would be so much better. We just have to wait until the policy is announced and see how to do it.

Xizeng and Er Mao get up at half past five every morning and go jogging along the Bund to the Garden Bridge and back. They do that twice and then come home.

A few days ago, Er Mao introduced a girl to Xizeng, but Xizeng didn't like her. He said she wasn't pretty enough. We'll just have to wait and see. If you can move back to Shanghai, it'll be easier to talk to the kids about things like this. But we have to be patient. I still have to write to Lezeng and Guobin. They wrote saying they'd received the peanuts.

More news soon!

All my best,

Meitang

※

July 23

Dear Pingru,

I received the ten jin of grain coupons and your letter. The day before yesterday the housing officers came around and wanted me to pay 345 yuan. The total is 1,245 yuan, less 800, so there's three hundred or so to pay off, at ten yuan a month. I said I can't pay it, and they said in that case, we'll have to move to a smaller apartment, but I don't want that either. Obviously, they were extremely unpleasant. They said I shouldn't act like that when I owed rent, I hadn't learned anything. They threatened me. I just let them talk and ignored them. . . .

It's incredibly hot this year in Shanghai though it's gotten a bit better recently. Mother's very frail in her old age, and a few days ago she had a dizzy spell in the morning. Luckily Xizeng and I hadn't set off to work yet, and we got on the phone to Maotou and asked him to come (he goes to work at six). But by the time he got here, she'd improved. Maotou thought it might be low blood sugar. He gave her some sugar water and she felt a little better. Then the day before yesterday, she fell again, but luckily it wasn't so serious. It's a real headache but thankfully this time it was in the morning too. Otherwise, with no one in the house, what would she do? She doesn't listen to me when I tell her not to walk around so much. The last few days, she's been keeping still, maybe because she's sore from the bruises, and she doesn't want to get a scolding from us. I've been having problems with my heart lately because I'm so worried, it races, then it calms down in a while. So I've been taking care to get enough rest. With Maotou out so much, there's more to do in the house. Saturdays and Sunday evenings, Yunhong always goes to the movies with her friend, and I can't tell her not to go. Maotou does two night shifts a week. Xizeng mops the floor and cooks for me on his days off. In this hot weather, I wash the clothes every day so there's always a lot to do. Well, I'll stop now. You look after yourself in this hot weather. I'll write again soon.

All my best,

Meitang

❄

September 25

Dear Pingru,

Thank you for your letter of September 18, and all your news.

I've been rather low in spirits recently. We've heard that our community workshop is going to retire all the workers at fifty-two years of age. It'll probably begin next month.

They're going to deduct the rent I owe starting at the end of September. If I have to retire, I'll be ten yuan short a month. The back rent and the current rent comes to sixteen yuan a month, so I won't be able to cover the household expenses. It's terribly upsetting. I don't know how long your problem's going to go on for. It'll be okay if you can get back to Shanghai. For the children to get married, they need money. It doesn't matter what they say in the newspapers, how on earth are they supposed to get money? Right now, they need more food and other things than before. Young people are vain about their appearance. And as soon as any girl hears how bad off we are, she wants nothing to do with us. It doesn't matter how hard you look, you'll never find a young person who doesn't mind about their standard of living. On top of that, if I'm retired, it'll be worse. The children are getting older every year, that's why it's so upsetting.

However, I've put on a little weight. It's still hot in Shanghai. This time last year it was much cooler. We didn't buy anything special for the Midautumn Festival, but Maotou brought 1.5 yuan's worth of pig's liver from the hospital, Lezeng spent 2 yuan on sausages and a few jin of pears, and Xizeng bought ten mooncakes when he got off work. Then Peizhi's mother sent over eight Cantonese-style mooncakes, which was very embarrassing. . . . Anyway, we had a good Midautumn Festival, and Lezeng bought a little wine too, which looked good on the table. National Day will be here soon and we get three days off. I heard they're economizing on fireworks this year and there will be no parades, but next year will be thirty years since 1949, so there will be big celebrations.

Last night, we watched *A Spy in the Eastern Harbor,* and it was quite good. I'm feeling low at the moment and I went to sleep afterward. Tonight, *Dream of the Red Chamber* will be on again, and the children are thrilled. They can't get enough of it. There are supposed to be some good films around—I've seen all the ones made in China, but the foreign ones, like *The Counterfeit Coin, Fidelity,* and *The Hunchback of Notre Dame,* are excellent. There are two Chinese films that are due to be screened soon, *Ashima* and *Five Golden Flowers.* The star of *A Spy in the Eastern Harbor,* Da Shichang, is very handsome, and apparently all the girls write him letters. He was Dr. Fang in the film *New Shoots in Springtime* and Lin Yusheng in *The Young Generation.* Have you seen it?[36]

It's Sunday today, and I've got the day off. Lezeng's at home so I'm not too busy and I can write to you.

Is it nice and cool where you are? You must be busy at work. . . . I'm going to do the washing, so I'll stop now.

All my best,

Meitang

October 16

Dear Pingru,

I got your letter of October 8 and the five yuan, thank you.

In your last letter, you spoke about writing to the Education Bureau. We all talked about it and we feel it doesn't make sense. . . . You want to get into foreign language teaching but although they're short of foreign language teachers, the places where they really need them are in the provinces outside Shanghai. There's not much chance that the Education Bureau will allow you to transfer back to take a teaching job. There *is* a possibility that you can get your old job back, because there's a justification for that. I'm not sure what you would put in a letter to the CPPCC; you could draft it, and tell them about the letters you've written to the United Front Department and the Education Bureau. . . .

Lezeng is getting ready to return to Yichun at the beginning of next month, and he'll try to get transferred back to Shanghai on medical grounds. What a pity we have no money, otherwise he'd be able to bring a set of furniture with him—he'd get permission, coming back on medical grounds.

Our jobs go on pretty much the same. Maotou is working very hard. As soon as he gets back home, he buries himself in study books and listens to foreign language radio programs. He doesn't watch TV and is much thinner than he used to be. Yunhong has got thinner too, and looks sallow, I don't know why. She eats only half a bowl of rice and she seems depressed. I've told her to go and get herself checked out. . . . I've put on weight but I still feel low. I'm ready for bed by seven every evening. Sometimes I go to sleep in front of the TV. A few days ago, we watched *The Million Pound Note,* a satirical comedy based on the Mark Twain short story. It's very good, have you seen it? There have been quite a few films of Chinese operas on lately, the Peking opera *The Legend of the White Snake,* the Shanxi opera *Taming of the Princess,* the Cantonese opera *Panfu,* the Huangmei opera *Fairy Couple,* and so on. They're very popular. The spy film *The Black Triangle* is good too.[37]

Are you busy? Do you still have to spend your evenings after work tutoring? You're not getting any rest, you should take more care of yourself.

We're fine, don't worry about us! I'll write more soon.

All my best,

Meitang

October 31

Dear Pingru,

I've had your letter for a week and have only gotten around to replying today. You must have been looking for it every day! I know how busy you are, and how stressful work is. . . .

It's all right if you don't come home this Spring Festival. I'm afraid I'll be retired in the New Year. If you come back when I'm retired, I'll be at home to keep you company.

Lezeng won't have an answer to his application to come home on medical grounds until next year. . . . We talked about you writing that letter. I still don't know the best way to present it but I think you should emphasize things like the hardships you've faced. . . . It's all very well me saying that, but if I had to write that letter, I wouldn't know how to put it either. As soon as we talk about this stuff, I get upset.

Maotou has a night shift tonight and won't be back, because he doesn't have a thick quilt. He doesn't have a padded jacket either. It gets so cold in the suburbs. It's really not good, him going out early in the morning and coming back late at night without a padded jacket. We'll just have to wait until it gets really cold and then see. . . .

I've been watching all the satellite broadcasts of Vice Chairman Deng Xiaoping's visit to Japan. Some Japanese films have been shown too. The best one is *Manhunt*. Then there are two Mexican films, but they're no good at all. Don't go and see them. *Family* opens today in Shanghai and it will be on TV soon.[38] We have a TV so we can watch at home. Tickets to good films are really hard to get.

About Xizeng getting a girlfriend, he's way too picky. She has to have a good job, he won't consider any girl who works in a service job like a hotel or restaurant or hair salon or factory canteen, let alone a community workshop. He's a strange boy. But I have no money so I can't say anything.

Are you in good health these days? There was a power cut today and I rested, then made the most of it and wrote to you.

All my best,
Meitang

※

November 17
Dear Pingru,

I received your letter of November 5 a while back.

Lezeng has bought his train ticket and leaves at five o'clock tomorrow afternoon. Maotou and Xizeng are both at home so they can take him to the station. Guobin wrote asking me to buy five jin of sugar to send with Lezeng, so he can give it as presents. I had to do that, so that means the ten yuan of back rent won't get paid this month.

In the October 7 *Liberation Daily,* in an article about professionals getting their old jobs back, it says that the provisions for releasing people sentenced to Reform Through Labor apply to anyone who's served their term doing Reeducation Through Labor too. Get hold of a copy and look. Then on the fourteenth, there was a very good article in the *Wenhui News,* which said: "Democracy must be strengthened and the rule of law must be instituted." And another yesterday said: "We must seek the truth from the facts, wrongs must be righted." And today there was one saying that rightists should be rehabilitated; you have a look at them. There are articles like this every day now.

As for writing your letter to the CPPCC, I don't think it is likely to do any good. The children say that it would be better to write to the Procuratorate, or the newspaper. You'll have to make your circumstances clear. . . . Be bold, there are some things that must be said. Isn't this the time to "seek the truth from the facts"?

Maotou has been rather low recently because the medical personnel in the hospital are taking exams. He's a nurse so can't take the doctors' exams. He went and asked them but they said no. They said he had stated in his letter that he wanted to work as a nurse, so he could take only the nurses' exams. When the director of nursing found out, she told him he should try his utmost to get a university place. Each one of our children has had problems because the family's "class origin" is bad. I'm enclosing twenty jin of national grain coupons and twenty jin of Shanghai grain coupons. Just send them back if you can't use them.

All my best,

Meitang

TOP "The Old Couple": "The old couple, the old couple / Old dreams, never ending / Old accusations, unresolved / Old stories without end / Love that never dies."

—In imitation of my cousin Dahe

BOTTOM "Happy memories / The cherry-apple tree blossoms / Traces of one's past life / The years passing"

—"The Eve of the Dragon Boat Festival," 2009. Written by Pingru, age eighty-eight

CHRONOLOGY

	Pingru and Meitang		China
1921	Spring		The Beiyang government is divided by struggles between rival factions; Sun Yat-sen becomes president of the government in Canton (Guangzhou)
	July 23		First Congress of the Communist Party of China (CPC) in Shanghai
1922	November 27	Rao Pingru born in Nancheng	
1924	January		First United Front between the CPC and Sun Yat-sen's party, Kuomintang (KMT), known as the KMT-CPC Alliance
	April		Central Huangpu (Whampoa) Military Academy established; National Revolutionary Army (NRA) commanded by Chiang Kai-shek formed there
1925	March 12		Death of Sun Yat-sen; Chiang Kai-shek establishes himself as head of KMT
	April 14	Birth of Mao Meitang	
1927	April 12		The Shanghai Massacre, end of the First United Front; beginning of the civil war between KMT and CPC
	August 1		Nanchang Uprising, the Chinese Red Army is formed
1928	December 29		End of Beiyang government: Chiang Kai-shek establishes government in Nanjing
1931		Pingru's family moves to Nanchang city	
	September 19		Japan invades Manchuria
	November 7		Mao Zedong creates the Chinese Soviet Republic in Jiangxi
1934			The NRA attacks the Chinese Soviet Republic; beginning of the Red Army's Long March
1936	December 12		KMT and CPC form Second United Front against Japan; truce in the civil war

	Pingru and Meitang		China
1937	July 7		Beginning of the Sino-Japanese War
		The Meitang family moves to the French Concession in Hankou	Japan occupies Peking, Tianjin, then Shanghai
	December		Nanjing massacre; Chiang Kai-shek's government flees to Chongqing; the Huangpu Academy is transferred to Chengdu
1940	March		Installation of a collaborationist government in Nanjing: the Reorganized National Government of the Republic of China
	August		The Eighth Route Army launches a large-scale offensive in the north of China; the Japanese pursue a scorched-earth policy in retaliation
	Fall	Pingru is admitted into the Huangpu Academy (based in Chengdu)	Japan joins the Axis Powers
1941	April 13		The Soviet-Japanese Neutrality Pact
	December 7		After Pearl Harbor, the Allied Forces lend support to Chiang Kai-shek
	December 25		Japan occupies Hong Kong
1942	Fall	Pingru's mother dies	
1943	February	Pingru joins the 100th Army of the NRA	
	May		The Japanese attempt to take Chongqing and inflict heavy losses on the NRA in Hubei
	November	Battle of Changde	Chinese victory at Changde
1944	April		Operation Ichi-Go: the Japanese take Changsha, Liuyang, Hengyang, Guilin, and Liuzhou
	June	Battle of Hengyang	Beginning of the recapture of Chinese territory
1945	Spring		West Hunan Campaign
	August 9		The Soviet-Japanese Neutrality Pact is broken; the USSR invades Manchuria
	August 15	Japan surrenders	

		Pingru and Meitang	China
		Meitang goes to live in Linchuan	
	September	Pingru is a lieutenant in the 83rd Division	Nationalist troops attack the Communists in Shanxi; Chiang Kai-shek attempts to negotiate with the USSR with the aim of surrounding the Chinese Red Army in Manchuria
1946	Spring		Breakdown in Chongqing negotiations between the KMT and CPC; resurgence of the civil war
	Summer	Pingru and Meitang are engaged in Nanchang	The PLA Communist guerrilla movement extends to the south; Nationalist desertions increase
	Winter	Pingru and the 83rd Division arrive in Linyi	The Chinese Red Army becomes the People's Liberation Army (PLA)
1947	Summer	Battle of Menglianggu	The KMT loses the support of the Americans and of the Chinese population
	September		The PLA achieves a series of victories
1948	July	Pingru is on leave in Nanchang	
	September 17	Pingru and Meitang are married	
	October	The couple leaves for Xuzhou, then returns to Linchuan	The PLA takes control of Manchuria and Shandong, then of Beijing and Tianjin
1949	January 22		Chiang Kai-shek resigns from his post as president of the Republic
		The couple travels to Anshun	
	October 1		Mao Zedong declares the foundation of the People's Republic of China (PRC) in Peking
	December	Pingru and Meitang go to Guiyang, then return to Nanchang	The PLA lays siege to Anshun. The government and KMT supporters escape to Taiwan
1950	March	Pingru and Meitang open a Chinese noodle store in Nanchang	The PLA takes control of the west of China
	April 29	Birth of their son Xizeng	

		Pingru and Meitang	China
	June		Land reform: expropriation and redistribution of the land
	August	They close their store, Pingru looks for work	
	December	The family moves to Shanghai	
1951		Pingru works at the hospital and at Dade Publishing	
1952	February	Birth of their son Shenzeng (Guobin)	Anti-capitalist campaigns
	Summer	The family moves to number 18, Xin Yong An Road, Shanghai	
1953	February	Birth of their son Lezeng	First Five-Year Plan
1954	October	Birth of their son Shunzeng (Maotou)	
1955			Agriculture cooperatives are set up (First Great Leap Forward)
1956	January	Birth of their daughter, Yunhong	
		Dade Publishing becomes a national company, the Shanghai Health Publishing House	
	Summer		Agricultural crisis; problems appear in agricultural production
1957	February		Hundred Flowers Campaign
	Summer		Anti-Rightist Movement
1958			The Great Leap Forward (Second Five-Year Plan)
	September		The Shanghai Health Publishing House is integrated into the Shanghai Science and Technology Publishing House
	September 28	Pingru is sent to a labor camp in Anhui	

	Pingru and Meitang	China
		The Cooperatives are formed into People's Communes The Three Years of Natural Disasters begin
	April 27	Liu Shaoqi becomes president of the PRC, Mao remains head of the CPC
1960		Meitang is employed in a community workshop
1961		Liu Shaoqi criticizes the Great Leap Forward
1966		Beginning of the Cultural Revolution
1967		Beginning of the movement to send educated youth to the countryside
1968	October 31	Liu Shaoqi is removed from the presidency
1969		Shenzeng (Guobin) and Lezeng are sent to the countryside for reeducation
1971	October	The twenty-seventh UN General Assembly votes to include the PRC
1973		The "Gang of Four" comes to prominence
1976	September 9	Death of Mao Zedong
		Arrest of the "Gang of Four"
		Hua Guofeng becomes president of the PRC
1978		Beginning of reforms and the rehabilitation of the right wing
	December	Hua Guofeng loses power and position, Deng Xiaoping resumes leadership of the CPC
1979		Educated youth return to the cities
		Beginning of globalization
		The People's Communes are gradually dismantled
		The One Child Per Family policy introduced
	November 16	Pingru returns to live in Shanghai

	Pingru and Meitang		China
1980	February	Birth of Rao Yuanyuan, the son of Shenzeng (Guobin) and Chen Peizhi	
			With the backing of Deng Xiaoping, the government organizes economic reforms
	December 19	Pingru returns to his original post at the Shanghai Science and Technology Publishing House	
1982	June 20	Pingru is operated on for pancreatitis	
	December	Birth of Zhang Bing, son of Yunhong and Zhang Weide	Adoption of the fourth constitution, still in effect
1983	July	Birth of Rao Xingchao, son of Xizeng	
1984			Creation of special economic zones in several regions including Shenzhen
1985	November	Birth of Rao Shu (Shushu), daughter of Lezeng	
1987	January		Hu Yaobang steps down as secretary general of the CPC; Zhao Ziyang becomes secretary general
1989	April 15		Death of Hu Yaobang
	June 4		Tiananmen Square political turmoil
		Meitang is diagnosed with diabetes and uremia	Zhao steps down, Jiang Zemin becomes secretary general
1993	March 27		Jiang Zemin becomes president of the PRC
1997	July 1		The United Kingdom returns Hong Kong to the PRC
2003		Pingru and Meitang relocate to the suburbs of Shanghai	

	Pingru and Meitang	China
	March 15	Hu Jintao becomes president of the PRC
2004		Pingru undergoes a coronary bypass
		Meitang shows signs of cognitive impairment; Pingru begins administering Meitang's daily dialysis
2008	March 19	Death of Meitang in Shanghai
	May 12	Earthquake in Sichuan
	August	Summer Olympic games in Beijing
2010		China becomes the world's second-largest economic power
2013		Publication of *Our Story*

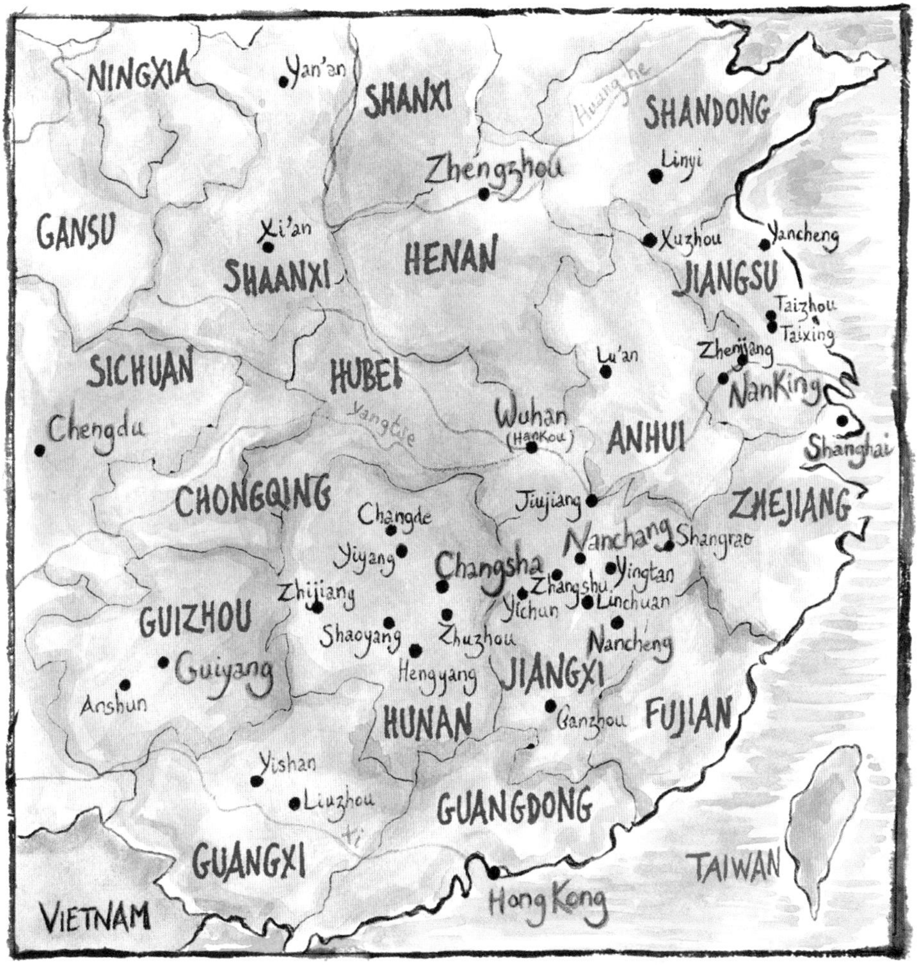

NINGXIA
Yan'an
SHANXI
Huang he
SHANDONG
Zhengzhou
Linyi
GANSU
Xi'an
Xuzhou
Yancheng
HENAN
SHAANXI
JIANGSU
Taizhou
Taixing
Zhenjiang
SICHUAN
HUBEI
Lu'an
NanKing
Wuhan
(HanKou)
Yangtse
Chengdu
ANHUI
Shanghai
CHONGQING
Jiujiang
ZHEJIANG
Changde
Nanchang
Shangrao
Yiyang
Changsha
Yingtan
Zhangshu
Zhijiang
Yichun
Linchuan
GUIZHOU
Shaoyang
Zhuzhou
Nancheng
Guiyang
Hengyang
JIANGXI
Anshun
HUNAN
Ganzhou
FUJIAN
Yishan
Liuzhou
GUANGDONG
GUANGXI
TAIWAN
VIETNAM
Hong Kong

NOTES

1. A fable in *The Analects of Confucius,* relating the childhood of a disciple of Confucius and his filial piety toward his stepmother who treated him unjustly, notably in providing him with nothing but rags to wear during winter.

2. Refers to a poem by Zhang Ying, Grand Secretary of the emperor Kangxi, written to resolve a demarcation dispute between his family and his neighbors. "The emperor Qin Shi Huang left us the Great Wall, but the Wall did not stop him from leaving us": these lines from the poem, according to the anecdote, inspired each family to leave the other with three feet of land so that a six-foot-wide alley appeared between their residences.

3. The prefix "old" (*lao*) followed by the surname is a common way of designating or addressing someone close, no matter his age.

4. The author is quoting the first verse of a poem written by Du Fu following the announcement of the surrender of general An Lushan's rebels in 763 AD.

5. The courtesy name was used because it was considered improper before 1919 to address someone by the name given to them by their parents. The tradition persisted in well-to-do families until 1949. According to Mr. Rao, this provided him with the name he uses (Pingru), the name given at his birth being Zhaoyang.

6. Mi Fu (1051–1107) was a famous painter and calligrapher, born in Xiangyang in Hubei.

7. Yue Fei (1103–1142) was a celebrated general who fought under the Southern Song dynasty against the Jin invaders.

8. Inspired by the poem "Lute," by Li Shangyin (813–858).

9. Hankou is today part of the city of Wuhan, the capital of Hubei. After the second Opium War (1856–1860), five foreign concessions were established in Hankou, one of which was the French Concession (which lasted from 1896 to 1943).

10. On July 7, 1937, the Japanese soldiers who were training near the Lugou Bridge (known in the West as the Marco Polo Bridge) realized that one of their men had disappeared and demanded the right to search homes in the neighboring city of Wanping. When the Chinese troops opposed this demand, the Japanese opened fire. The incident triggered the Sino-Japanese War.

11. The Central (Whampoa) Military Academy of Huangpu was founded in 1924 by Sun Yat-sen and transferred to Chengdu during the Japanese invasion.

12. This is from Mao Zedong's version of a poem by Saigo Takamori (1828–1877).

13. A song by Jiang Kui (1152–1220) that describes the city of Yangzhou as it was devastated after the attack led against the Southern Song dynasty by the Jurchens of the Jin dynasty in 1161.

14. From Meitang's favorite song, sung to the tune of "Auld Lang Syne" and written for the Chinese version of the film *Waterloo Bridge* (1940), starring Robert Taylor and Vivien Leigh and directed by Mervyn LeRoy.

15. Dates on the wedding invitation follow the traditional Chinese lunar calendar. Pingru and Meitang were married on September 17, 1948, in the modern calendar.

16. The *yamen*, residential and administrative headquarters of officials during the imperial era, designates by extension public offices or the bureaucracy.

17. Ouyang Xiu, a Song dynasty poet (1007–1072).

18. The author is referring to *qianzhuang*, sometimes translated as "native banks," private traditional banks that disappeared in mainland China after 1949.

19. In its complete form the saying goes: "Eat in Guangzhou, dress in Suzhou, frolic in Hangzhou, and die in Liuzhou."

20. Li Bai (Li Po, 701–762), "Nocturnal Reflections."

21. This verse by Xu Hun (788–860) is frequently cited to describe the tense climate preceding a conflict.

22. The *hukou* is a certificate of residence that records members of a household. This system was created at the beginning of the 1950s with the intention of controlling the movement of the population.

23. The Dade Hospital (the Hospital of Great Virtue, named after a passage from the *Yi Jing* [*I Ching*, or *Book of Changes*]: "The great virtue of the sky and the earth is called life"), specializing in obstetric gynecology, was founded in 1937 by Yang Yuanji

and his wife, Zhang Yuling. They then extended their organization to include health education, midwifery, and publishing. In 1956 Dade Publishing was integrated into Shanghai Health Publishing House, which in 1958 became the Shanghai Science and Technology Publishing House.

24. Shenzeng and Shunzeng are Pingru and Meitang's second and fourth sons, respectively. The romanized spelling is almost the same so, to avoid confusion, they are referred to throughout by their family nicknames, Guobin (Shenzeng) and Maotou (Shunzeng).

25. Xizeng was born in April 1950, so by Western reckoning he would be eight, but traditionally the Chinese reckoned a baby's age as one year old at birth.

26. Literally, production groups (*shengchan zu*), which were created in the cities during the Great Leap Forward in 1958 and primarily employed housewives for their manual labor.

27. These alleys, called *lilong*, formed a typical residential neighborhood in old Shanghai. In the 1960s, the neighborhood committees became the primary units of the Communist Party organization in this city.

28. These words are from the classic opera *Taking Tiger Mountain by Strategy* (1969).

29. This is the Chinese version of the Japanese song "Kitaguni no haru" (1977) by Sen Masao.

30. Shen Fu, *Six Records of a Floating Life* (1877).

31. Extract from a poem by Li Shangyin (ca. 813–858).

32. The Jiangxi Huaguo Mountains are the fictional place where the Monkey King, Sun Wukong, reigned in the classic novel *Journey to the West*. Many sites were named in this manner in China.

33. This film by Zheng Junli (1959) portrays the imperial official Lin Zexu (1785–1850), who

opposed the opium business in Canton between 1838 and 1840.

34. Yan Jizhou's *Ye huo chun feng dou gu cheng* (*Struggles in an Ancient City*, 1963) explores the Chinese Communist resistance during World War II. *Man yi bu man yi* (*Satisfied or Not?*, 1963) is a comedy in the dialect of Suzhou. *Sentinel Under the Neon Lights*, taken from the eponymous play by Shen Ximeng, is the story of a division of the People's Liberation Army that resists the sirens of liberal ideology.

35. *Nü jiao tong yuan* (*The Undercover Female Agent*, 1978) is a film by Qin Fusheng that narrates the acts of resistance in the Kuomintang in 1947. *Man yuan chunse* (*Ah, It's Spring*, 1961) is a comedy written in the dialect of Shanghai with Zhou Bochun and Yao Mushuang.

36. *Donggang die ying* (*A Spy in the Eastern Harbor*, 1978) is a movie by Shen Yaoting. *Hong lou meng* (*Dream of the Red Chamber*, 1978) is one of several serial adaptations of the great classic of Cao Xueqin. *The Counterfeit Coin* (1955) is a Greek film directed by Yorgos Tzavellas. *Wafaa* (*Fidelity*, 1954) is an Egyptian film by Ezzel Dine Zulficar and Abdullah Barakat. *Notre-Dame de Paris* (*The Hunchback of Notre Dame*) is a French film directed by Jean Delannoy in 1956. *Ashima* (1964) and *Wu duo jinhua* (*The Five Golden Flowers*, 1959)

are based on short stories, the first concerning the Yi ethnic group and the second, the Bai ethnic group. Xie Jin's *Chunmiao* (*New Shoots in Springtime*, 1975) and Zhao Ming's *Nianqing de yi dai* (*The Young Generation*, 1965) were revolutionary propaganda films.

37. *The Million Pound Note* (1954) is a British comedy by Ronald Neame based on the short story "The Million Pound Note" by Mark Twain. *The Legend of the White Snake* (*Bai she zhuan*) and *Marriage of the Fairy Princess* (*Tian xian pei*) are popular Chinese short stories that have been the basis of a number of adaptations: here Meitang is referring to the Hong Kong film directed by Yueh Feng in 1962 entitled *Bai she zhuan* and the filmed play *Tian xian pei* with Yan Fengying and Wang Shaofang (1955). *Da jin zhi* (*Taming of the Princess*) is a classic of the Shanxi (*jinju*) opera, while *Panfu Suofu* (*The Interrogated Husband*) is part of Shaoxing (*yueju*)'s opera repertoire. Finally, *Hei san jiao* (*The Black Triangle*, 1977) is a Chinese film by Liu Chunlin and Chen Fangqian.

38. Jun'ya Satô's *Kimi yo fundo no kawa wo watare* (*You Must Cross the River of Wrath*, also known as *Manhunt*, 1976) was one of the first foreign films to be shown in China after the Cultural Revolution (in 1978). Chen Xihe and Ye Ming's *Jia* (*Family*, 1957) is the adaptation of the eponymous novel by Ba Jin.

ABOUT THE AUTHOR

Rao Pingru was born in 1922.
He lives in Shanghai, China.